"BETWEEN INNOCENCE AND WISDOM, LIVE A LIFE THAT MAKES BOTH PROUD."

SOMEONE WITHIN YOU

[SOMEONE WITHIN YOU]

Publisher: Pushkar Patil

ISBN: [978-93-5779-633-0]

Disclaimer: This book is self-published by the author. The concept of looking inward and exploring the hidden self is a theme shared by many authors and speakers across different works. However, the views, vision, and ideas expressed in this book represent the author's own perspective and unique approach to inner exploration. All edits have been made by the author, with the primary intention of inspiring readers to look positively within themselves and to help them discover their true self.

Printed in India

SOMEONE WITHIN YOU

From Author,

Hello dear readers,

It is such an asynchronous communication where I am writing and you are reading this book in your comfort space, expecting that you will learn something new after reading it. As high as your excitement is, in the same way I am feeling while writing this book, because this topic *"Someone within you"* is really special for me. It is a concept, rarely spoken about but observed in everyone, and it has literally changed my perspective on how to look at someone. There is a person inside you who is totally different from the one you show outside, but still a part of you. Some of you may dislike that inner person, but someone like me will adore them.

In your daily basis of life you are someone's friend, son/daughter, family relative, good neighbor, love. These are the roles which you are playing in your life as a person showcasing relation you have with person. But what about you? In same way you also have a relation with yourself and these relation doesn't depend on feeling as observed when emotions change person also change but in this case it's just like a person living in you your true identify whose purpose is to push you ahead in life, be with you all the time.

This book is helpful in many ways, by:

- **Providing Vision:** An author does not only write books, but anything that is written begins with thoughts, not just words. Words are simply a means of communication, like letters that carry your message. Reason why a vision is necessary to see yourself.
- **Identifying the Person in You:** After you gain the vision, you should know what to look for in yourself. There might be some bad sides as well as good ones. You don't have to make a decision immediately your job is simply to see and accept that this side exists in you.
- **Accepting and Implementing:** When you are certain about your inner side this person inside you—you have to accept it in any form, because that is reality. Everyone is built differently. Even the strongest man may contain a sweet side within him. We may not know it, but he knows it. That is not weakness, that is strength.

All these points we are going to cover in this book. Your journey of transformation begins here, dear readers. After reading, your vision towards yourself will change. You will get to know your true hidden side, which might feel like a quite different, but only you know about it no one else does. How to use it and where to use it for your benefit, all of this you will learn in this book. So get ready, and let's start.

"YOUR GREATEST STRENGTH LIES IN YOU. WHEN YOU HONOR YOUR WORDS, SUCCESS BECOMES UNSTOPPABLE."

TABLE OF CONTENT

About the book

Before reading you all should know what this book is about and what does this book contain and most important what will I achieve after reading this book?

There is a presence inside you that is constant, unchanging, and quietly guiding you through every moment of your life. This presence is what I call the "Someone Within You." It is not a stranger, it is the most authentic version of yourself the observer behind your thoughts, the calm presence behind your emotions, the silent witness who remains steady even as circumstances shift around you. Meditation and self-talk is the doorway through which you meet this inner companion, and once you recognize it, your relationship with yourself and the world transforms.

The Someone Within You is the essence of your identity, stripped of roles, masks, and expectations. In daily life, you play many parts: student, parent, professional, and friend. Each role demands a certain behavior, a certain mask. But beneath these masks lies the true self, the one who watches, listens, and feels without needing to perform. Meditation allows you to peel away the layers of identity until you encounter this core. At first, the encounter may be subtle a whisper of intuition, a fleeting sense of calm but as you practice, the voice grows clearer. You begin to recognize patterns, the way your inner self encourages you.

Meeting the Someone Within You is like meeting a lifelong friend you had forgotten. You realize that you are never truly alone. Even in moments of despair, there is a presence within that offers strength. Even in moments of confusion, there is a voice that offers clarity. This realization is profound because it shifts your source of guidance from external to internal. Instead of seeking validation from others, you begin to trust yourself. Instead of fearing rejection, you begin to accept yourself. Instead of feeling lost, you begin to feel guided.

Meditation is the practice that makes this meeting possible. In silence, you create space for the inner self to emerge. The noise of daily life fades, and the subtle voice becomes audible. This voice does not shout, it whispers. It does not command, it suggests. It does not criticize, it guides. Listening to it requires patience, trust, and openness. At first, you may doubt it. You may wonder if it is real or if you are imagining it. But over time, as you act upon its guidance and see the results, your trust deepens. You realize that the Someone Within You is not a fantasy but a reality, a presence that has always been there, waiting to be acknowledged.

The Someone Within You is practical, not abstract. It influences your decisions, your relationships, and your actions. When you consult this inner guide, decisions become easier because they are aligned with your values. Challenges become less daunting because you draw strength from within. Relationships become more authentic because you no longer seek validation outside, you have found it inside. This inner dialogue is not mystical, it is deeply human. It reminds you that growth is not imposed from outside but shaped from within.

How often people feel torn between what they want and what others expect. This conflict arises because they ignore the Someone Within. They listen to external voices society, peers, and family while silencing the inner voice. Meditation restores balance. It teaches you to listen inward before acting outward. It reminds you that the most important approval is your own. When you act in alignment with the Someone Within You, you feel peace, even if others disagree. When you act against it, you feel unrest, even if others applaud. This is the measure of authenticity: living in harmony with your inner self.

The Someone Within You also provides resilience. Life is full of challenges loss, failure, rejection, uncertainty. External support may not always be available, but internal support always is. The inner self offers comfort in despair, courage in fear, and stability in chaos. It reminds you that you are stronger than you think, wiser than you believe, and more capable than you imagine. Each life session becomes a reminder that you are not alone, that you carry within you a source of strength that cannot be taken away.

This inner presence is also a source of creativity and inspiration. Many artists, writers, and thinkers describe their best ideas as coming from within, as if whispered by an unseen guide. This is the Someone Within You speaking, offering insights that the conscious mind cannot generate. Understanding yourself enhances this creativity by quieting the noise and allowing the inner voice to be heard. In silence, ideas flow, connections emerge, and inspiration arises. The inner self is not only a guide but also a creator, shaping your destiny through imagination and vision

The Someone Within You is timeless. It is not bound by age, circumstance, or achievement. Whether you are young or old, successful or struggling, the inner self remains constant. It is the part of you that has witnessed every moment of your life, from childhood to adulthood, from joy to sorrow. It carries the memory of your experiences, the wisdom of your lessons, and the clarity of your truth. Meditation allows you to access this timeless presence, to draw upon its wisdom, and to live in alignment with its guidance.

Ultimately, the Someone Within You is the foundation of destiny. It is through this inner presence that you discover your path, your purpose, your calling. Destiny is not imposed from outside it is shaped from within. It may not provide a map, but it offers a compass. By following this compass, you shape a destiny that is authentic, purposeful, and fulfilling.

In closing, the Someone Within You is not a concept to be understood but a presence to be experienced. It is the most authentic version of yourself, the guide who knows your truth, the companion who never leaves. Once you recognize it, your life changes. You live with clarity, strength, and authenticity. You realize that you are never alone, that you always carry within you a guide, a mentor, a friend. And in this realization, you find peace, purpose, and destiny.

INTRODUCTION

OUTER PERSON

We all go through different phases in life where we feel calm, anger, fear, sadness, surprise and many more. These are basic human feelings that we experience daily. But the question arises, do they affect our true behavior?

What is true behavior?

If you ask a normal person, they will be likely to define true behavior as what we see through a person's actions, body language, and the quality of language used in communication. This is important, no doubt. But is that the complete answer?

Maybe it's partially true, but from an author's perspective, the scenario is entirely different. When we talk about the *outer person*, we are referring to the behavior someone shows to the world. The whole game is about perspective. Reading this book from a reader's perspective means you are just looking through your own eyes. But if you change your vision and think like an author, you realize that an author writes through his thoughts, not by his words.

For better understanding, let's take an example: Anish is a 10-year-old boy who believes his whole life revolves around studies. From his perspective, this is true because his schedule is packed: school from 8 a.m. to 2 p.m., coaching from 4 p.m. to 6 p.m., and homework at night. He barely has time for himself during the week, except on Sundays.

It was observed that Anish's behavior on Sundays was completely different from the rest of the days. Not only his behavior, but even his personality seemed to change. That's because he finally had time for himself he played with his friends and enjoyed life, which transformed him, even if it was for a day.

Sometimes what we want and what we get more like expectations versus reality play a big role in shaping our mood and behavior. You must have noticed this in yourself. When you want something and you get it your feelings are at the peak of happiness. But the moment you realize you won't get it, your emotions drop like a free-falling body. For hours, your mood remains off, and even if someone tries to interact with you, you don't give your 100%. That's because you've lost your outer character a personality you usually carry or let's say energy.

At the start, we discussed the common definition of behavior which is: actions, body language, and communication skills. These are characteristics of the outer person, but they don't always matter. For example, if someone doesn't have strong communication skills, can we judge them as not being true to themselves? Absolutely not. In fact, we should praise them for being real.

One of my friend who struggles with speaking English. He can write well, but when asked to explain or present something, he often gets stuck something commonly observed in beginners. But what I admire most about him is that he never steps out of his character. Keep yourself at his place, now you are given a task to present a PPT in front of a professional person and you know your English communication is weak especially on stage, what would you do in this situation? Some people would write a script and memorize it, while others might give up. But my friend believed in himself. He stood on stage confidently and presented his work. Yes, he got stuck many times, but he still managed to speak. By doing so, he proved he was loyal to himself, he believe in himself and kept his actual behavior true in front of everyone.

Understanding outer person is quite easy as compared to inner person. Other people judge you by what you show them, but they don't know anything about your inner side.

It's only you who knows what you are going through. There's a quote which I personally follow a lot for myself.

"At the end of the day, it's you facing yourself with reality in your hands."

The moment you realize the depth of this quote your perspective towards outer person will get clear. In daily basis we are surrounded by many people which include family members, friends, neighbors, strangers, but the moment of truth comes to create your own identity in life and to prove yourself you will find your almost every friend is busy with their own life so you have only you. Yeah they are with you to support you at your lows, but you must learn to handle yourself in life. Your friends and family are supporters who will provide you rope to climb the mountain rest everything is on you. Handling situations and fighting is never going to end the only person you will have till end of journey is you.

Are you capable of climbing the mountain? This question you should ask yourself or your inner person. Which I call as "Someone Within You".

Why to be dependent in life if you have someone within you who is ready to help you all the time. Face the problems instead of avoiding or running away inner person is like your brother always there like your right hand. There is a famous line which I have listened. No matter how many people surround you family, friends, colleagues, or strangers the ultimate confrontation is always with yourself. Others may walk beside you, they may support you in moments of weakness, but they cannot live your life for you. The responsibility of shaping your identity, of carrying your choices, rests entirely in your hands. This realization is hard to accept because it strips away dependency. We are conditioned to lean on others, to expect rescue, to believe that someone else will spoon feed or carry our burdens. But the truth is, when the night grows quiet and the world fades into silence, it is only you who must face the mirror. That mirror does not lie. It reflects your decisions, your failures, your victories, and your resilience. And in that reflection, you discover the "Someone Within You" the inner person who has always been ready to guide you.

Avoidance is the greatest enemy of growth. Running away from problems does not erase them, it only postpones the confrontation. Life demands courage, not escape. There is a famous line: *"You can't run away from yourself."* Wherever you go, your inner person follows. The fears you bury, the doubts you suppress, the mistakes you deny all of they remain with you until you face them. The act of facing reality is not punishment, it is liberation. It is the moment when you stop hiding and start healing.

The inner person thrives when you choose responsibility over avoidance. It is the quiet voice that urges you to stand firm, even when the world feels heavy. It reminds you that strength is not measured by how many people support you, but by how deeply you can support yourself. This is not to dismiss the value of companionship, friends and family are precious but their presence is supplementary, not foundational. The foundation is you.

Think of life as a journey through a forest. Companions may walk with you for a while, but there will be a phase where you must walk alone. In those moments, the forest examines you in all ways. It whispers, will you panic in the silence, or will you listen to the rustling leaves and find guidance? The "Someone Within You" is that guidance. It is the compass that points you forward when no one else is around.

Facing reality also means embracing imperfection. You will make wrong decisions, you will stumble, and you will doubt yourself. But each mistake is a teacher. Each failure is a lesson. The inner person does not demand perfection, it demands honesty. Honesty with yourself about where you are, what you feel, and what you must change. When you stop pretending, you start progressing. Dependency weakens the inner person. It convinces you that your strength lies outside of you, in someone else's approval or support. But independence awakens the inner person. It teaches you that you are capable of carrying your own burdens, of solving your own problems, of creating your own identity. This is not isolation it is empowerment. It is the realization that you are never truly alone, because the "Someone Within You" is always present.

At the end of the day, when reality is in your hands, you have two choices: To avoid it or to face it. Avoidance leads to stagnation things starts to collect at a place just like a bunch of files on desk and suddenly one day when you get serious of your work those stack increase your pressure and stress instead face each problem one by one at right time it leads to transformation. The inner person is your ally in this confrontation. It gives you courage when fear whispers, strength when doubt shouts, and clarity when confusion clouds your vision. So, do not run. Do not hide. Stand in front of the mirror of reality and meet yourself. In that meeting, you will discover that the greatest companion you will ever have is not someone from outside it is someone from inside. And once you embrace that truth, you will never again fear being alone, because you will know that the "Someone Within You" is enough.

"How far you will run from the problem? The moment you will look back you will see it again."

Face the challenges they aren't for your bad, instead they are for your benefit to upgrade you in life. The more you will face yourself the reality will kick you how you are in reality, you expect some people to behave good with you in life. But have you ever asked question to yourself why the person isn't behaving properly with you but good with others? You might have some problem in you which you are trying to avoid because it's hard to accept that we contain some flaws. Keep that ego aside of I am perfect and accept how you are. You will love yourself, but some people won't love that one quality in you we are talking about outer person here. For better understanding some people won't like how you look, some might not like how you behave in public. These are your habits of outer person which can be changed and you should. The first thing people judge is all by outer appearance and behavior.

At a point in life everyone must face that reality slap about yourself. No one is born with perfection everyone learns from experience just like you. Every day is a learning day, something's you don't know till yesterday but you got a time to understand about it today, obviously it's for your benefit just take a step ahead, give yourself a personal interest to learn about the topic. Today my plan was to visit book festival in our city so I could have some new books in my shelf and gather some knowledge. But unfortunately the festival wasn't started yet yeah I was disappointed as I drove so far and left empty hand so I calmed myself down from getting upset and me and my friends made a plan to visit temple. After taking blessing we went for shopping and before going home we decided to eat ice cream. So while eating ice cream suddenly I got to know by friend is investing money in SIP monthly since a year. So at that place the first thing I did was thanked to nature. The plan of book festival wasn't fixed but after driving so far I came back empty hand what did I achieve and I got my answer it was about investment. Can you see the dots connecting which nature created my profit was not in those books but knowing about investment while eating.

Everything happens at perfect time you don't need to worry about it, it will come to you without fail at any unexpected time, the only thing you have to do is understand it and understand yourself. Everyone's goal in life is different but to achieve it you have to understand yourself first, go through the battles where you have to control yourself, control your mind from getting distracted and bring back to its place and forcefully make it work. Everyone's goal in life is different, but to achieve it you must first understand yourself. These battles of daily challenges you go through against distraction, doubt, and fear of failure, all these will come whenever you take decision of achieving some goal in life. These are like unexpected guest but can't avoid them. Once in your life you must have experienced this, when you are focused on your goal to achieve or to complete it, people around you start giving advice, some even silently hate but still act as if they care. Your efforts are seen by people through your outer personality only. You must have seen some who work silently on their goals, and you don't even know about it though you meet them daily, because they understand the power of keeping individual goals private. The famous superstition of the evils eye everyone has heard of when we share our happy life or goals we are chasing, or whatever good things we are doing that benefit us, suddenly everything collapses like the ground disappeared beneath our feet. At such times the most common human behavior is to say someone's evil eye caught me so I fell. But they won't agree they overshared about their goals if they believe in the evil eye. If not, they should claim it as nature's plan to teach something analyze the scenario and accept failure was to teach you a lesson.

Understanding the inner person is not easy because your inner self is hidden and only you know about yourself, but your outer self is exposed, so you must maintain boundaries to remain in the good region of others. Everyone has goals in life, everyone is busy, so expecting something in return from others is not valid. Once I was watching a video of Premanand Maharaj, and he said, **"If you love someone, just love them with your full heart. Don't expect anything in return. If the other person doesn't love you, no worries keep loving."** In the same way, when you are working on your goal, don't expect anything in return. The right people will come at the right time your job is just to start the process. I saw a beautiful video where a man wanted to take his sheep across a river. There was a wooden log acting as a bridge, but none of the sheep dared to step ahead. So the man tied one sheep with a rope and pulled it across. The others watched and gathered courage to cross, and one by one they all did.

In the same way, you just take the step ahead. Don't expect anything from others they also have their work, but they are with you. They will take huge steps if they see you taking one. The human mind skips hard work and it loves what is easy because it is wired to conserve energy and avoid discomfort. It's like electrons flowing in a circuit think of a parallel path, one with high resistance and another with zero resistance. Obviously, electrons choose the path of zero resistance. In the same way, humans do this, and it is natural behavior that comes first. But if a longer path contains more resources, humans will think, and most will choose the longer path.

Since our goal is to understand the outer person, people will easily judge you by your thinking and decision-making ability. People judge you instantly, not by words alone but by the clarity of thought and the strength of decisions a person carries. Decisions are mirrors through which others see your character. Be free, calm, and flow like water, clearing obstacles as if they are nothing. The greatest ability on earth among all creatures that humans have is thinking ability use it to its potential. Whatever work you do daily, do it smartly. Sometimes reducing effort is not the ultimate goal instead doing it perfectly matters, even if it takes effort. Still, the calmness behind work is appreciated.

Let's look at this concept with an example:

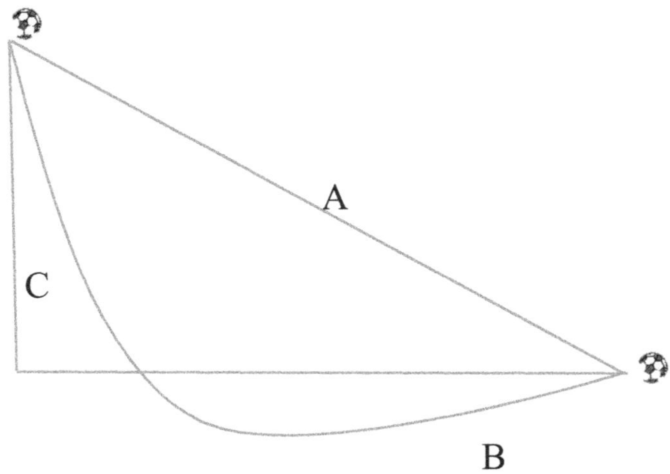

Brachistochrone curve

Most of readers must be familiar with this curve one of the best experiment of mathematics and physics where a ball have to move from top point to low point but it has 3 path A, B and C. At the exact same time 3 balls were released each ball following each path. Before looking at actual result let's see what human mind thinks about result.

According to human psychology, human mind only see's path A and path C first as they are original ones. Mathematically A is the shortest in distance compared to C but we also have to consider physics a moving body under gravity influence in that case C will be the fastest. But the one who tries to find another path which provides benefits mathematically and physics as well, will be the one winning this race same applied to life. **The brachistochrone curve proves that the shortest path between two points in a given space is not always a straight path.** Instead, it is a curve that minimizes the time taken to travel between the two points under the influence of gravity as well.

Now understand this same concept but change your perspective to understand the concept of outer person. An actual behavior of a person is influenced by his/her way of choosing path in life which may lead to change in personality or characteristic of a person but my goal is to show you the real path which is brachistochrone curve, which is important in life for shaping the real you.

The *outer person* means the actual you your normal behavior, the way you usually interact with everyone. That is your true behavior. A persons behavior is identified by the situation person is facing in real life, notice how some people change their behavior when they are in stress, constantly focusing on one goal and avoiding distraction for better focus and on other hand a person who doesn't care whatever be the situation still his/her behavior will be the same as the person shows in all phases of life.. This is what true behavior or outer person means. Who says emotional instability or life problem changes a person? If the person knows how to control ourselves and take decisions calmly by accepting all events occur for a purpose is the person won't get distracted and that's for sure.

A single decision can change everything.

One of the best lines, a single decision can change everything. Every decision you take it might be choosing a good college, job, partner, friends anything it might be, somewhere you are providing direction to yourself. Everything is already written by nature and we can't go beyond natures plan and that's true. If a particular event is decided by nature to play in your life, it will happen you can't deny and you can't run from it. Just like me I started writing because of a purpose and that purpose nature gave me like take it buddy it's for you. I was confused what is this? Nature is giving me but am I capable to do it by my own? And suddenly I got my answer as the author arrived in my life as I mentioned earlier about it in acknowledgment.

One day suddenly I had a thought while reading book why am I only consuming content if I can create by all the experience I have and the knowledge I have and in this way my life changed it was a turning point from where this line came, a single decision can change everything.

In same way when you are working on a project, yourself or you are figuring out yet. Your life will be like brachistochrone curve where you will have two paths A and B making you confuse what should I choose? In the diagram both path are taking you towards same path as life is totally unexpected, nature will always make sure you are on your way towards your written destination and on nature's path as well.

For nature it doesn't matter which path you will choose A or B, it will always make sure you keep walking and never give up because in the end you will stand at your destination written by nature as per your outer behavior, inner nature and karma how you treat yourself and others who are in your life.

Here's a diagram for your better understanding.

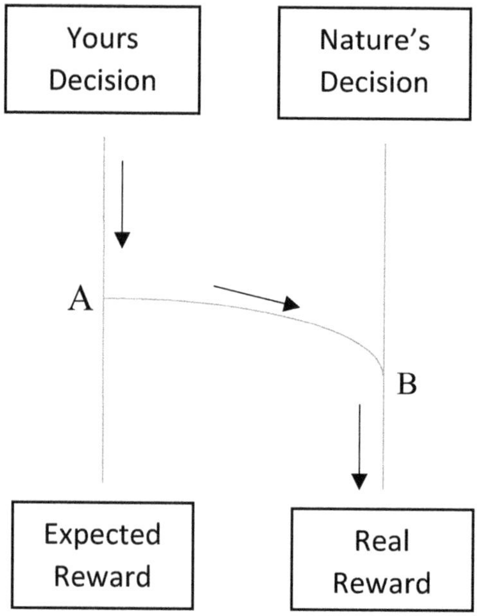

Decision Diagram

This decision diagram is a clear representation of how we humans take decision in our life and how nature changes it as per the reward written in our life. Brachistochrone curve is just an example of how a human should choose a path in his/her life which is smallest and fastest among all other routes available. But when you take any decision in your life make sure you know every decision you take will always change your life and that's for sure. Have a look in above diagram which contains four blocks.

First block which is your decision block it represents your present state you are living in where you are thinking about which path I should chose for better reward and success. Every person expects after giving 100% into a particular task I should achieve success and that's not true even you know about it. You have to fight for your reward, ever heard of those lines for success you have to sacrifice your sleep, give off everything people say these lines feel good as motivation that's true, but in reality those sleepless nights shows your madness for your goal when someone is so eager to achieve that thing sleep becomes a regret for that person, why am I sleeping my time is getting waste I need to work.

And here comes second block which is nature's decision. One thing I follow personally is nature always have something beautiful for you always, even the things you are chasing today because of those temporary happiness you get from it, stop chasing. Surrender yourself to nature and if you don't, just believe in nature everything will happen as per natures plan and that's true.

Look in diagram and let's say a person is taking a decision in life and mostly we humans take wrong decision and still we manage to be in a good place in the end every asked why? You will get this question's answer further for now let's go back to our topic, let's assume the person took wrong decision which is path A which he started following and the person doesn't know what he is doing is actually ruining his own career as he's ultimate focus is on the expected reward which is in front just like blinded from side and can see only in front.

Here enters nature in the game, as I said earlier nature always have something beautiful for you so when the person reached point A he's life was diverted toward second path which is parallel to his expected path so in this phase of switching path nobody can recognize or feel that this is not your actual path as per your plan, there is someone who is making sure you travel through good path not with the one which actually harms you and that someone is nature. When the person travels from point A to point B he's focus shifts to real reward which nature wants he should achieve. Now as a reader many questions must be going through your mind why will nature help me? If nature helps everyone then why everyone doesn't achieve success/real reward? That's actually good question, as I said nature will make sure you aren't travelling on path which is not for you so nature will add a bridge on your path so you cross and start walking on path which is for you. Nature won't help everyone that's a bitter truth, if you want nature should help you like it did to me you should have some qualities in you which are acceptance, understanding and surrender. In Someone Within You which is inner person main topic of this book we are going to talk about acceptance, understanding and surrender in detail. Inner person is the main topic for which I am writing and without acceptance and understanding it's impossible to have your inner person with you, for now let's talk on surrender.

When we move beyond the blocks of the diagram, the real essence lies not in the mechanics of decision-making but in the philosophy of how life unfolds. The diagram is a symbol, not a map it shows us that our choices are only half the story, while the other half is written by nature which we cannot control. What matters is how we respond to this natures plan.

Every human being begins with intention. You decide, you plan, you chase. But intention alone is fragile. Life is not always a straight line, instead it bends, it curves and it surprises with unexpected turns. The bend from point A to point B is not a mistake, it is the hidden wisdom or hidden key which opens new door. What you thought was failure is actually a new start for you transformation. What you thought was loss is often the doorway to something greater. The real reward is not always visible at the start, but it becomes clear when you look back and realize that the path you resisted was the one that shaped you most deeply.

This is why qualities like acceptance, understanding, and surrender are not optional instead they are essential. Acceptance teaches you to stop fighting reality. Understanding allows you to see meaning in detours. Surrender gives you peace in walking the unknown road. Together, they transform the way you experience life. Without them, you remain trapped in frustration, struggling to achieve expected reward. With them, you discover the real reward is often richer, deeper, and more lasting than expected reward.

The inner person someone within you is the compass that helps you recognize this truth. It is the part of you that sees beyond ambition, beyond temporary happiness, beyond illusions. When you start walking on wrong path your inner self warns you by giving small hints, in this moments you feel like something is wrong. The inner person whispers that the real reward is not about material success but it's about alignment with your-self. When you nurture this inner compass, you begin to see that even wrong decisions can lead to right destinations, because nature bends your path toward growth.

Think of life as a river. You can fight against its current, exhausting yourself, or you can flow with it, discovering landscapes you never imagined. The current is nature's decision, the bends are its wisdom, and the destination is the real reward. Your role is not to control the river but to learn how to travel with awareness. The more you resist, the more you suffer. The more you trust, the more you grow.

Summary:

This is the deeper lesson of the diagram where decisions matter, but they are not the whole story. Nature's guidance matters too, and it often carries the greater wisdom. The expected reward may satisfy your ambition, but the real reward will satisfy your soul and the inner person is the one who can recognize the difference. So, as you walk your path, remember life is not about perfect choices, it is about how you respond when the path bends. The bend is not failure it is design. The real reward is not always what you wanted, but it is always what you needed. The someone within you is the one who will help you see it. This is the flow of existence decision, diversion, reward, and realization. It is not a straight path, but a curved one and in that curve lies the beauty of your journey.

Message from Author:

Believe me readers whatever you do in life it might be of starting a new journey, new life, new goals, and new relations. Remember the decision diagram. There is a famous line, "First make something, and then make it beautiful." In same way when you start something just believe in yourself and believe in nature, just start the process nature will take you towards your written path where you should belong, never resist, never doubt natures plan just follow it. In the end you will end at place which you dreamed of today.

The Outer Person and the Curve of Life

An outer person is really shaped by the actual behavior of the inner person. How are your thoughts assigned towards your surroundings, people around you, and energy around you determines your outer person. Inner person is explained in detail in next chapter as the whole book is written on inner person itself but understanding outer person is must first look for the tragedy outer person is influenced by inner and for inner person your outer behavior decides your quality from inside. It is not like both for each other, imagine you are surviving in an un-habited area and you met a stranger who has an inbuilt skill of survival same like you. At that particular moment for both of you to survive you need to be together and help each other by the skills you have more like sharing but in reality you aren't meant to be in contact as you are stranger you decided to be together because other person have something you need and other person needs something you have. In same way is inner person and outer person both just need each other because they have something which other needs.

Human's life is more shaped by the outer person because we need to live in a surrounding or society in a group. Humans behavior is easily identified by observation how person behave, by looks, soft skills, manners which we can call as basic ethics and you also must have noticed this whenever we meet a new person initially we change our personality to professional so a proper image of our is maintained in mind of other person which is outer person and as time flows and we get to know each other slowly-slowly we become comfortable and our inner behavior which we hide initially slowly comes out and we get to know each other so well that we spend whole day with that person.

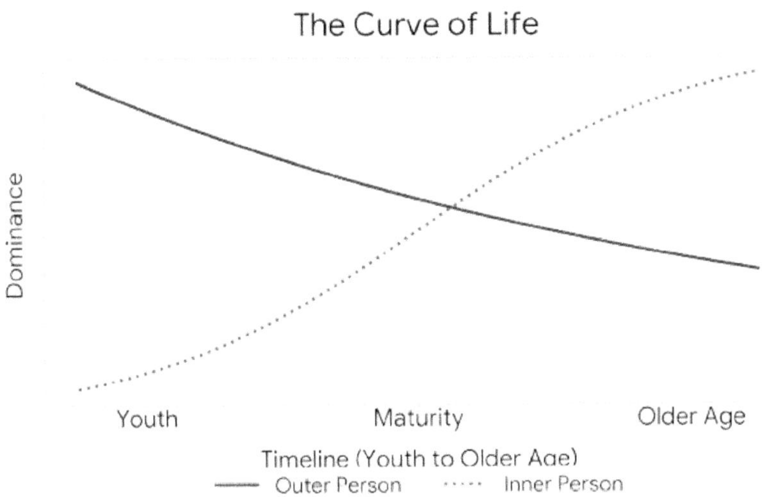

The curve of life is shaped by how well we balance these two. If we rely only on the outer person, we risk becoming hollow, defined only by appearances. If we rely only on the inner person, we risk becoming isolated, misunderstood, or unseen. The true art is in weaving both together presenting an outer person that is respectful, ethical, and socially aligned, while nurturing an inner person that is authentic, imaginative, and deeply alive. This balance is what creates character. It is what allows us to survive in society without losing ourselves, and to nurture ourselves without losing society.

As we grow older, the curve of life bends differently. In youth, the outer person dominates where we are eager to impress, to be accepted, to belong. We polish our manners, rehearse our words, and hide our vulnerabilities. But as maturity arrives, the inner person begins to demand space. We realize that authenticity matters more than appearance that depth matters more than breadth, that trust matters more than performance. The curve bends inward, toward self-awareness, toward the realization that the outer person must serve the inner, not suppress it.

The “Someone Within You” is the bridge across this curve. It is the hidden companion that ensures the outer person does not become a mask too heavy to carry, and that the inner person does not become a secret too lonely to bear. It whispers balance be professional, but be authentic, be polite, but be truthful, be social, but be selective. It reminds you that the outer person is the image others see, but the inner person is the essence you live. Together, they shape the curve of life, bending it toward growth, resilience, and meaning.

So when you think of the outer person, do not dismiss it as superficial. It is the necessary face of survival in society. But remember that behind it lies the inner person, the one who gives the outer its quality, depth and truth. The curve of life is the dance between these two, the gradual unfolding of masks into authenticity, of strangers into companions, of appearances into essence and in that dance, the “Someone Within You” is always present, guiding, balancing, and reminding you that life is not about choosing one over the other, but about harmonizing both to climb the mountain of existence with dignity, wisdom, and joy but for better understanding let’s have a look at other factor of outer person which are important to shape a good person externally which are,

1) Surrounding
2) People around you
3) Energy around you

I. Surrounding:

If you are into non-fiction topic like me a minor detail you must have observed is any author who write on topic self-help and productivity always mentions about surrounding.

My favorite book ATOMIC HABBIT by James Clear mentions about surrounding, *Motivation is Overrated, Environment often matters more.*

No matter how much you try to motivate yourself, your surrounding plays an important role in shaping your identity. When you are studying you should create environment such a that you feels like you are studying if not change your surrounding visit library and have a focused environment. But it's not that simple there are other minor factors also which influence your productivity. Create your surrounding as per your work if you are studying keep only books on desk for easy future access avoid distraction keep your electronic devices far from you increase your friction to achieve distraction so you're focused on your work which is close to you.

In short when you manage your surrounding your ability to focus on work increases when eliminating distraction and keeping your tools in your vision you are focused on your goals your mind doesn't waste energy in fighting with problems instead it tries to avoid them initially or else ignore the distraction like they never exist. This increases focus naturally your body also adapts this behavior change in you where you are giving a proper undisturbed time to your work, due to this change a person gets a habit many author call it as habit formation.

Repeated Focus = Habit Formation

Each time you focus on your work it creates a rhythm and that's called consistency and once consistency is created in work it is followed in habit and turns human into discipline. Your mind forces you to do productive work it becomes a habit your brain see reward in a long run and also benefits you which you are getting in long run.

Whenever a person is disciplined these changes are observed directly at person's mentality and physical self. Because discipline directly changes inner person its focus is simple change inside automatically outside person will change just like attack at weakest point of a tree which is roots. Observe a disciplined person how his consistency is steady, punctual notice his ability to stay on task without being distracted, discipline is shown only under pressure as they have trained themselves to add resistance to problem.

As internally a person is independent by habits who is neither controlled or being controlled all decisions are self-made. Reason why you see a different person outside and different person inside. Once Zlatan Ibrahimovic said, *"My philosophy is why be normal when you can be best.*

That's a good question why? I can't understand why some people are lazy, when you have lot of work to do if you are free just work on yourself, learn and upgrade. Once you start following the process of upgrading yourself and learning daily you will get addicted to it trust me I am not saying this because I have to write. When I am writing this book I am also learning daily before I sleep I plan my next day and when I wake up I go through schedule that saves my time and before writing I have already researched what I have to write today even some topics which I don't know about I gather information and understand the whole concept at that moment itself. There are many days where my whole day went in research and I haven't wrote a single word that day just because I need to deliver a good self-help book to my readers so they understand the concept properly. My aim is only to give you something you are in search for if you are reading this book it's all because nature wants you to read this book.

You might be in search of questions in your life, maybe you'll get your answer through this book even a single person's life will change because of this book I will be happy and that's enough for me.

II. People around you:

You must have heard this quote in your life, "Surround yourself with people who take you ahead, who have same goal, same mindset as you, because these are one which understands the importance of growing in life. In a room full of rich people you will find only rich."

There's a rule which says, *"Be with the person who is ahead of you, who is at higher post than you. You will learn lots of thing from experience the individual have gained."*

Being with right people actually plays an important role in shaping your identity, because choosing right people will take you in right direction those people who know where to invest time and where to avoid are smart players. As we talked about surrounding being with right people gives you an environment to grow, it gives you challenges, a right amount of knowledge which is necessary, a vision to look at your goals, consistently hustling, and most important never stopping and upgrading daily. You get addicted to be the best version of yourself daily. People around you act as casting which shapes you when a molten iron is poured in mold. Here the molten iron is all important skills which you need in your life to achieve your goals. In surrounding topic the boy kept books on table and kept distraction far away, here those books are important tools needed for goals, in same case here those tools might be skills, knowledge and a right path.

Once you are shaped as a strong mold you are unshakable, because your outer mold is created, but one which is inside is created with discipline and clarity makes you unshakable. Even a mold can be broken when a person is surrounded with wrong people. These "Wrong Company can weaken your foundation." Surrounding yourself with right people brings right strength they don't only make you grow in one direction but make sure you expand in multiple but in correct one. Even science says we unconsciously mirror the behaviors of people we spend time with. Their discipline becomes our discipline, their vision becomes our vision.

People around you are not just companions in your journey, they are the invisible forces shaping your identity, your habits, and ultimately your destiny. The quote "surround yourself with people who take you ahead" is not merely advice, it is a principle of life that determines whether you grow or stagnate. When you are in a room full of people who share your vision, your hunger, and your discipline, you find yourself naturally propelled forward. Their mindset becomes your mindset, their discipline becomes your discipline, and their vision becomes your vision. This is because human beings unconsciously mirror the behaviors of those with whom they spend time with, and so the company you keep becomes the mold into which your potential is poured.

Just as molten iron takes the shape of the mold it is casted into, your skills, talents, and dreams take shape according to the environment you choose. If the mold is strong, you become unshakable but if the mold is weak, your foundation cracks. Surrounding yourself with the right people means surrounding yourself with challenges, with knowledge, with clarity, and with vision. It means waking up each day with the urge to upgrade yourself, to hustle, to never stop, and to become addicted to being the best version of yourself. The right people don't just comfort you, they push you, they stretch you, and they force you to grow beyond your limits. They remind you that success is not born in comfort but in challenge, and that growth requires discipline and persistence. Wrong company, on the other hand, weakens your foundation, normalizes mediocrity, and distracts you from your goals. It makes excuses seem acceptable and lowers your standards without you even realizing it. That is why choosing your circle is not optional, it is essential. Your environment is never neutral it is either pulling you forward or holding you back.

Every person around you is either strengthening your mold or breaking it. When you are surrounded by people who value growth, you will naturally begin to value growth. When you are surrounded by people who waste time, you will unconsciously waste yours too. This is why successful communities often produce clusters of success. In a room full of rich people, you will find only rich, not because wealth itself is contagious, but because the mindset of wealth is. They talk about opportunities, discipline, investments, and vision. Their conversations themselves are lessons, their actions are silent mentorship. Being in such an environment means you are constantly learning, constantly upgrading, constantly expanding. Once your identity is shaped by discipline and clarity, you become unshakable. Your outer mold creates your habits and routines protects you, but your inner mold creates your value and vision makes you truly strong. Even storms cannot break a foundation built on clarity. The right company ensures you grow not just in one direction but in multiple, and in the correct ones. They help you balance ambition with wisdom, hustle with patience, and vision with humility.

We mirror the discipline, habits, and even emotional states of those we spend time with. If your circle values fitness, you will likely adopt healthier habits. If your circle values learning, you will read more, think more, and grow more. In the end, people around you are not just companions, they are co-creators of your destiny. They shape your identity, fuel your growth, and strengthen your foundation. Choose them wisely, because your future is being molded every single day by the company you keep around you.

III. Energy Around You:

One of the best concept or factor which really influence outer person, an extraordinary even if you implement this in you others would be influenced by you and that's for sure. Here energy doesn't mean any spiritual energy actual energy we are talking about energy which is seen through eyes, which is felt and which is experienced which is called as AURA.

i. Energy Seen Through Eyes

It's my experience which I observed when I was sitting in a common room open for all public, anyone could come, sit, do their work, eat, talk, and spend time. I was chilling in the room and spending time, but personally I felt bored as the actual energy that creates vibe was missing. Suddenly my friends arrived, and I felt happy as someone was beside me gossiping and sharing memories. But for some point, I was quiet because, as I said about people around you, these weren't the ones who actually give you a kick in life they were average ones who mold themselves when they want based on mood or else remain normal.

So everything was fine, going with the flow, and after some time one of my friends arrived who changed the environment with the energy he showed us. He entered with properly dressed clothes, perfectly ironed and tucked-in shirt, pure leather belt, trimmed beard, and settled hair. His presence made everyone feel low appearance is first impression, and surely his appearance turned the energy around, making the topic into class. The way he grabbed everyone's attention made them feel their level. Imagine you are in his place and you enter a room where people admire your appearance, how will you feel? Well, being practical, real ones will mirror you, and the next day you can see them maintaining proper dress code. This is what I meant. Your presence may change another person's path. Even if you meet someone for the first time, your appearance creates an image in their mind they won't forget. As the famous quote goes, "First impression is the last impression." Your outer character reflects in another person's mind just by looking at you, creating an impression of discipline and classic living. A man who maintains himself understands the meaning of dominating an environment by small changes. A small change in daily life can bring a bigger change by year's end.

In one of the podcast I heard this, if you want respect, then respect your body first. Respectfully build your outer self, your physical body, because that's the first thing people observe your outer person and you are judged by it. The very first form of respect comes from here. There were two friends who spent the whole day together. One was fat and another one was fit. Talking about mental ability, both were above average. But the fat friend was criticized for his appearance everywhere he went. Even when they met new people, most people start conversations with the fit one first. It wasn't his fault that he was fat or the other was fit. When you care for your body through fitness, grooming, or posture, you signal to others that you value yourself. That often translates into how they value you. The fit friend attracted attention first because people subconsciously associate fitness with discipline, confidence, and leadership, whereas the chubby friend, despite equal mental ability, faced bias because appearance triggers stereotypes. This isn't his fault its society's conditioning.

Humans are wired to notice physical cues before intellectual ones. It's a survival instinct rooted in evolution, appearance signals health, strength and social status. Every day you should wear classic dress. Here classic means if you are visiting a professional place such as college, company, or meeting. At such places I observed people often wear shirts but don't tuck them in with a proper belt and plain formal pants. If your body is fit here fit means natural, not too fat, not too slim, somewhere between average and slightly muscular like you exercise daily and you aren't wearing classic wear, you're missing something. The energy you should feel and the aura you are creating but not sensing. Whenever you step inside a room with proper wear as I described, with a trimmed beard and haircut that suits your face and body, you set an aura you haven't imagined. Others will surely observe you, and your physical appearance will set an image in their mind. So whenever they talk about you, automatically good thoughts, words, and positive feelings will come because you've already won the first battle by creating a good image.

Sometimes when you enter a room, it's not just about who is there but about the energy they carry. Science explains this through mirror neurons. These are tiny reflections in our brain that copy emotions and vibes of people around us. So when someone walks in with confidence, discipline, and strong aura, others unconsciously sync with that energy. That's why one person's presence can change the whole atmosphere. Along with this, there's the halo effect. It means if people see one good trait in you, like neat dressing or fitness, they automatically assume you have other good qualities too, like intelligence or leadership. This is how psychology silently works in the background while you're just being yourself.

Society also plays a big role in how appearance is judged. In sociology, there's symbolic interactionism. It says the way you dress or carry yourself acts like a symbol, and people interpret meaning from it. For example, a tucked-in shirt with belt and polished shoes doesn't just look professional instead it signals discipline and respect. But this isn't the same everywhere. In some cultures, casual dressing is seen as authenticity, while in others, formality is considered respect. So the energy you project through appearance is always filtered by culture.

Now think about leaders. Whether it's a military officer in uniform, a CEO in a suit, or a sports captain in their jersey, appearance is used as a tool to project authority and unity. It's not just clothing it's a strategy to influence people. Research shows employees are more likely to follow instructions from someone who looks confident and put-together, even if their authority is the same as others. This proves presence is not only personal it's also a leadership skill.

But presence isn't only about clothes. Non-verbal communication plays a huge role. Your posture, eye contact, tone of voice, and even the way you walk are silent signals people pick up before you say a word. Energy management also matters, speaking with calm confidence, walking with purpose, or wearing a subtle fragrance that leaves a lasting impression. And the most important part is consistency. If you show up well-groomed and disciplined every day, people build an image of you in their minds. That image becomes your personal brand, good things are spoken behind your back even when you're not around.

ii. AURA

Aura is one of the most famous words used to define the energy of an individual. It is commonly described as the energy field that surrounds a living being, reflecting their emotional, mental, and spiritual state. If understood properly, you realize that the true motive of the "outer person" is aura itself. Practically speaking, you don't need to create your aura instead, you need to understand its meaning and use it for your benefit. Rather than flexing, aura should be used to shape your identity.

Take the example of Virat Kohli, the Indian international cricketer. His discipline toward personal development transformed his entire life, making him one of the most famous sports celebrities. His aura is unmatchable. On the field, Kohli's aura is expressed through his intense body language. His actions radiate confidence, his aggression speaks his mind set and he is truly a man of his words. If he decides he will score a century, he does. If he decides to dominate his opponent, he does. This comes from being true to himself when your actions are so authentic that they are praised by others, you begin to create an image in their minds.

Fans idolize Kohli not because they want to become cricketers themselves, but because they aspire to his mindset and discipline. His aura describes his identity. Look at his sharp eyes, perfect posture, fit body, and communication skills top notch. He worked on himself. He managed his surroundings, drew boundaries, and committed to a strict diet aligned with his goals. He eliminated distractions and developed strong self-control. By refining small habits and ensuring that yesterday's mistakes were not repeated today, he became the person he is now. That is the essence of learning from mistakes.

Today, Kohli's aura is so powerful that not only his teammates but millions of Indians are inspired by his actions. This is what aura truly means. Have you noticed that whenever someone achieves greatness whether success, goals, or extraordinary feats they radiate aura. Aura is what others perceive when they think of you. They remember your achievements, your personality, and the energy you carry with your physical presence. It is seen through the eyes, felt deeply, and often hard to express in words.

Consider M.S. Dhoni. When he walks out to bat at the Chepauk Stadium, the sound level crosses 130 decibels. That roar is not just for his cricket it is the reflection of his aura. What he have achieved and what he gave to the country.

In the same way, you too must create an aura in order to establish your identity, a personality that everyone respects, protects in your absence, and celebrates in your victories. Let us return to the first page of the "outer person," where I spoke about the true behavior of an individual, revealed through actions, body language, and the quality of communication. But this is not always the case. As I mentioned earlier about my friend who lacks proper communication skills how then is his outer person true? The answer lies in being true internally.

Your physical body should carry meaning. When you walk, your presence should convey a message. This can be reflected in your appearance, which shows discipline in your work, which demonstrates consistency toward your goals or in your honesty, even in failure, which reveals loyalty to yourself. Ultimately, people will choose you because you possess something unique and powerful that others lack.

The main motive of the outer person is to be true, because in the next chapter we will explore the inner person. Remember, the outer person is a reflection of the inner person just as when you look into a mirror, you see yourself.

To illustrate this, consider the brachistochrone curve. In life, you are presented with three paths:

- **Path A** is straight but long. Its simplicity makes it the most common choice.
- **Path B** is longer and demands patience.
- **Path C** is different it requires vision. Though it appears risky as it curves downward, it is actually the fastest and most efficient path. Trust it, and you will strike your goal with precision, like a one-man punch delivered perfectly.

Be consistent, be focused, avoid distraction, follow people who take you ahead, improve yourself daily than yesterday, make appearance classy, maintain boundary, communicate healthy, respect other's, and most important be loyal to yourself. That's how your outer person character is maintained there are many ways to do so choosing correct path is important have a vision where you can see the matrix.

Aura is not only about how people see you in the present moment, it's also about how your energy lingers even after you leave. Have you noticed how some individuals walk out of a room, yet their presence is still felt? That's aura it's the invisible memory of your actions and discipline that stays behind. Aura is like a fragrance it doesn't vanish instantly, it remains in the air and reminds people of who you are.

Another important thing about aura is that it cannot be borrowed or copied. You can mirror someone's style, their clothing, or even their words, but aura is built only through your own consistency. It is the result of years of effort, sacrifices, and choices. That's why when people admire someone's aura, they are actually admiring the journey behind it. Aura is not a mask you wear, it is the reflection of your truth. Aura also has a magnetic quality. People are naturally drawn to those whose aura radiates confidence, discipline, or positivity. This is why some individuals attract opportunities, respect, and admiration without asking for it. Their aura works like gravity it pulls others closer. But this magnetism is not about luck. It is about the energy you cultivate daily. Every small habit, every disciplined choice, every moment of self-control sums to the strength of your aura.

There is also a protective side to aura. A strong aura acts like a shield, keeping negativity and distractions away. When your aura is high, people think twice before disrespecting you, because your presence itself demands respect. This is why aura is not just about impressing others it is about protecting your identity and maintaining your boundaries. When you build your aura, you don't just change how others see you instead you change how you see yourself. You begin to carry yourself differently, speak differently, and even think differently. Aura is the bridge between your outer person and your inner person. It is the proof that your discipline, your focus, and your loyalty to yourself are visible to the world.

- Aura as lingering presence (like fragrance).
- Aura cannot be copied, only built through consistency.
- Aura as magnetism that attracts people and opportunities.
- Aura as protection and boundary.
- Aura as transformation of self-image.

➤ **The AURA Circle:**

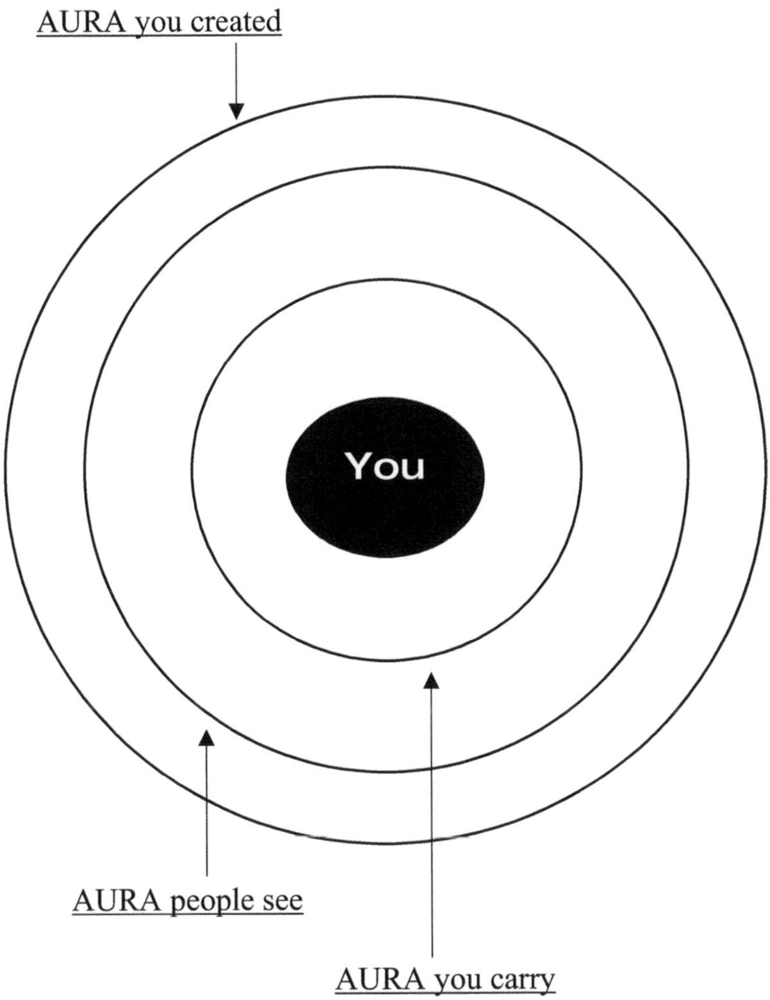

When we look at the diagram of aura the **You** at the center, surrounded by the aura you carry, the aura people see, and the aura you created it becomes clear that aura is not a single layer of energy but a journey of transformation.

Each circle represents a stage of growth, and together they form the identity that people remember you by.

1) At the core is **You**. This is the place where you stand. It is the place where discipline, focus, and loyalty to yourself begin. Without a strong center, the outer layers collapse. That is why self-love and self-respect are the foundation of aura. If you are not true to yourself, no matter how polished your outer appearance is, people will eventually see through it.
2) The next layer is the **Aura You Carry**. This is the energy you feel within yourself every day. It is invisible to others but deeply felt by you. If you wake up with clarity, discipline, and motivation, this aura is strong. If you carry confusion, negativity, or laziness, this aura weakens and shrink inside. Think of it as the fragrance you wear for yourself it sets your mood before anyone else notices. This layer is built through habits, consistency, and the way you talk to yourself.
3) Then comes the **Aura People See**. This is the impression you leave in the present moment. People don't see your thoughts, but they see your actions, your body language, and your communication. This aura is the reflection of your inner discipline. It is why some people inspire respect the moment they walk into a room. Their aura radiates confidence, focus, and truth. This is the layer where your inner energy becomes visible to the world.

4) Finally, the outermost layer is the **Aura You Created**. This is the legacy of your actions the aura that remains even after you leave. It is the memory people carry of you, the respect they hold, the image they protect in your absence. This aura cannot be copied or borrowed it is built only through years of effort, sacrifices, and choices. It is the invisible shield that protects your identity and attracts opportunities.

Most importantly, aura transforms how you see yourself. You stop doubting your worth because your aura reflects your truth. You stop chasing validation because your aura already commands respect. Aura is the bridge between your inner person and your outer person it is proof that your discipline, your focus, and your loyalty to yourself are visible to the world. So, if you want to build an aura that inspires, protects, and transforms, start at the center. Be loyal to yourself. Be consistent in your habits. Be disciplined in your actions. Respect others, but never lose respect for yourself. Aura is not about copying someone else it is about becoming so true to yourself that your presence lingers like a fragrance, long after you leave. That is the power of aura. That is how you create your identity.

INTRODUCTION

INNER PERSON

Now let's talk about inner person the main topic of this book. As far I hope you have understood the concept of book on what topic it is, and the outer person is so far clear let's go ahead.

Remember the quote in Outer person,

"At the end of the day, it's you are facing yourself with reality in your hands."

It doesn't matter who is with you in your life, in your long goal run, because at the end of the day you have to face yourself.

I was reading David Goggins' biography. He is a retired US Navy SEAL, ultra-marathon runner, and a motivational speaker. Goggins dreamed of being in the Air Force during his junior years. Those students who wanted to join the army had to give an exam, the Armed Services Vocational Aptitude Battery Test (ASVAB), in which David Goggins failed on his first attempt, as the passing criteria was to score 36 marks. He was a lazy boy in his childhood who used to skip hard work and choose an easy, less effort path. On the other side, his mother was still in emotional pain from Wilmoth's death, and she received a letter from school showing his reports scoring D grade, and it was sure if David didn't show any effort in his studies and attendance he would fail in senior years.

This was the first turning point of David's life. His mom didn't even scold, she didn't want any apology. It was complete silence and she was not speaking a single word. Silence in the room was speaking loud, something reality David was facing. Later that night David saw a poster of Michael Jordan and Special OPS in his room which stood as source of motivation to him. Then he went to take a shower and looked at himself in the mirror and realized the reality needs to be changed. The moment when he looked at himself in the mirror, a boy with no future, no purpose, just spending life without any efforts to chase dreams. At this point David was facing himself with reality in his hands. When David looked at himself in the mirror he didn't only look at his outer person but also his inner person was lazy as fuck. His inner person didn't accept him as he should be according to his goals. At that point in his life who was beside him? Only his mom, but she was supporting him externally. At the end of the day who was beside him? Nobody.

After looking at how David was physically and his reality was not as per his expectation, not even close, he grabbed his shaving cream and started shaving his head and beard, continuously taunting himself, and by the time he was completely shaven. At this point he was sure now I will control myself and do only those things which I want. His goal was only to fix himself physically and study to clear his (ASVAB) exam. After 2 failed attempts, at the third he finally cleared it. From where did this self-confidence come?

In Virat Kohli's case he looked himself in mirror blamed him for who he is, a boy who was not in shape not in discipline and decided to change himself and today what we see him is a man with his words who proved himself and changed himself from where all this came.

That's what I want to tell you readers. If you think you have a lot of friends who support you at any point when needed, that's good, but don't forget they are the ones who support externally. When you are down emotionally, they may understand you and lift you up, but it's only you who truly knows what you are going through.

At every success and at every failure in life, if you have grinded for hours, days, or even months and years for a single goal, it's only you who knows how much effort it takes to achieve the feeling of finally matching your expectation. People may be beside you celebrating, but it's only you experiencing the moment, living in the present, absorbing that energy, remembering those efforts and sleepless nights, those overthinking phases where questions arrived in mind will I achieve it all? And suddenly those moments finally came true. At this point all credit goes to your inner person who was with you all the time, constantly pushing you ahead, just another person living in you who never gave up at your worst, who was awake with you all those nights, who was motivating you at your lows. Thank yourself. Remember all your achievements in your life, what you did when you finally won while chasing your goals, how you felt. Remember that happiness, how you congratulated yourself at those wins.

The **inner person** is the hidden architect of your life it is the silent force that shapes your choices and defines your identity. Unlike the outer person, who interacts with society through manners, appearances, and impressions, the inner person is the one you face when the noise goes silent, when the crowd disperses, and when you are left alone with your thoughts. It is the companion that never leaves. What makes the inner person powerful is its dual role. It confronts you with reality and it empowers you with possibility. When you look in the mirror and see the gap between who you are and who you want to be, that confrontation is the inner person speaking.

1) The inner person is also the **keeper of your effort.** Others may celebrate your victories, but only you know the sleepless nights, the doubts, and the sacrifices. Only you know the grind behind the result. That knowledge is stored in the inner person, and that is why victories feel so personal. They are not just achievements they are conversations between you and your inner self, affirmations that the struggle was worth it.
2) Another dimension is the **relationship between inner person and self-belief.** Self-belief is not built by applause or validation it is built by the inner person reminding you of your worth. When you congratulate yourself after a win, when you pat your own back after a long day of effort that is the inner person affirming your value. It is the inner person saying: *I was with you through the grind, and now I celebrate with you.*
3) The inner person also teaches **ownership of identity.** Hurt, regret, and energy all flow through it. Hurt tests your resilience, regret tests your wisdom, and energy tests your focus. The inner person is the one who decides whether hurt becomes destruction or strength, whether regret becomes paralysis or wisdom, whether energy becomes waste or growth. It is the filter that transforms experiences into lessons

4) The inner person is also the **guardian of transformation.** Change does not begin when others motivate you it begins when the inner person confronts you. It begins when you stop blaming circumstances and start listening to the inner voice that says: *Control yourself. Fix yourself. Push yourself.* That is the moment when the inner person takes charge, and that is the moment when life changes.

At the end of the day, no matter how many friends support you, no matter how many people celebrate with you, it is only you who knows the truth of your journey. It is only you who faced the doubts, the grind, and the sleepless nights. It is only you who absorbed the energy of the moment when expectation finally matched reality. And it is only you who can thank the inner person the "Someone Within You" for never leaving, for never giving up and for always pushing you forward.

So, readers must understand the inner person is not a concept, it is a reality. It is the hidden companion who shapes your outer behavior, who pushes you through pain, who celebrates with you in silence, who confronts you in the mirror, who motivates you when no one else does. It is the "Someone Within You" who never leaves, who never lies, who never stops believing. And once you learn to listen, to nurture, and to trust this inner person, you discover that the greatest strength you will ever have was inside you all along.

Inner Personality

Every person living on this planet has different versions inside them for loved ones a different personality, for friends and family another. Observe yourself, how many times you switch your personality in a single day. That's not done manually, it's automatic, and it happens because of emotions. No one can control it everything depends on how close, how strong your bond is with a person.

Humans are like shape-shifters, or call them chameleons, who don't change colors but change personality to fit into their surroundings, to play their role, and to match energy. Its universal two people only meet and stay when their energy matches in some field. When your friends are in a room and you enter with your aura, notice how the rhythm and surrounding energy change, because people are in a state of adjusting themselves to match the energy and that's called as personality shifting. It provides a kind of safety, of not being the exception in a room where all others are the same and you are different. It's certain no one will accept it it's like others are south and you are also south, or vice versa, repelling each other.

Some readers won't accept or understand this, so let's look at nature around us. We know a tree only needs water and sunlight as its main source to grow, when the tree expands its root expand deep down in soil in search of water. In forests such as the Amazon, you will find trees tall enough to match buildings of 8 stories to even 25 stories, because they don't get enough sunlight when they are short whereas other trees block sunlight, which acts as an obstacle to new ones for growth. So, as per situation and survival, they also need to change themselves as much as they can just to survive. But take the same tree in another open savanna region its height is small compared to the ones in the Amazon, because at that place resources are easily available.

Now some readers will say, that's nature it all happens because nature finds its own way to survive in any condition. But think of the concept from human perspective, do humans have to change in every situation, in every room, just to match the energy? Instead, if they remain as they are, others would also remain as they are. Being true doesn't mean mirroring other people. This will reveal everyone's true side, making it easier for you to figure out who's the one here to rule, who's to dominate, and who is just being normal, not caring what is going on. A lot of things get clear by this simple act instantly analyzing the place by implementing a small change in us. As we know our own personality, understanding others also matters. As discussed in the outer person, people around you also matter.

Personality shifting is one of the most fascinating aspects of human behavior. As I said, we move through different versions of ourselves automatically, without conscious effort, because emotions and bonds trigger these changes. It's not manipulation it's adaptation. Humans are wired to adjust their energy to match the rhythm of the environment, just like a chameleon adjusts its colors to survive.

But here's the deeper truth, adapting is natural, **living only as a mirror of others can blur your identity**. If you always change to fit in, you risk losing the essence of who you are. That's why awareness is critical. When you notice yourself shifting personalities, pause and ask: *Am I changing because I want to, or because I fear rejection?* This simple reflection separates growth from compromise.

Think of personality like water. Water takes the shape of any container it adapts. But water also has its own properties. It satisfies thirsty person, it sustains life, and it carves valleys through persistence. In the same way, you can adapt to situations without losing your core truth. The goal is not to resist change, but to remain authentic while flowing through different environments. When you walk into a room with strong aura, others naturally adjust to your energy. That's influence. But if you constantly adjust to everyone else, you give away your power. True strength lies in balance knowing when to adapt and when to stand firm. This balance reveals the hidden dynamics of any group who dominates, who follows, and who remains neutral. By staying true, you become the mirror that exposes others' real selves.

Nature teaches us this lesson clearly. Trees in the Amazon grow tall to fight for sunlight, while trees in the savanna stay short because resources are abundant. Both adapt, but neither loses its identity as a tree. Humans too must adapt, but not abandon their essence. Your personality should be flexible enough to survive, yet firm enough to define your uniqueness.

So the challenge is this: **don't just be a shape-shifter, be a vision-shifter.** Adapt when necessary, but let your aura set the tone. Be the one whose presence changes the rhythm of the room, not the one who dissolves into it. This way, your personality becomes a tool of clarity you understand yourself, and you understand others.

Knowing Others

Your true identity, which resides within you but is hidden from others, plays a major role in shaping who you are and creating newer versions of yourself your new identity. People will give you time and respect only if your behavior is pleasant. Here, "pleasant" means calm, supportive, kind, and fun type qualities most people naturally admire and respect. Everyone expects respect in return, and while jokes among friends can be lighthearted, they must remain within boundaries so no one gets hurt. This defines a person's character an image formed in the minds of others.

For example, imagine a group of friends gathered in a room, enjoying themselves, partying, and catching up after a long time. One friend cracks a joke about another's personal matter. Some may laugh it off, but if the person targeted feels hurt, the joke has crossed a boundary. His mood changes instantly, and the joker's image shifts into an unsafe zone someone who doesn't respect limits. From then on, whenever that person enters the room or his name is mentioned, others may experience a personality switch in how they perceive him.

In such situations, if someone makes a personal joke at your expense, observe carefully. Yes, you should stop them to maintain your respect, but if they continue, don't let it drag you down. Instead, note the kind of person they are. Surround yourself with people who lift you up, not those who pull you back psychologically.

We never know how others will respond. Everyone expects jokes to be taken lightly, but expectations don't always match reality.

It is said and often proven that when a person is angry or jokes go beyond limits, they reveal their true personality. In anger, people rarely lie. Anger strips away self-control, removing the filter that normally governs speech. At such moments, the truth spills out, directly proportional to the intensity of the anger they hold inside. Like a snap of Thanos' snap, their restraint disappears, and what remains is raw truth unfiltered and unmasked.

Emotional Intensity = Perceived Honesty

All those spoken words hides positivity and mostly intent is to hurt other one by saying all facts which are true so those words are mixed with reality sometimes its complete true sometime partial.

Example: "You are careless!" but its partial way of expressing person's nature.

Same goes while cracking joke when someone goes personal you also crack a joke in order to make person to go wild mode which makes the person more angry and the truth will be revealed but in order to defend as you are against. They become so involved to defend that they mirror their inside identity which is your ultimate goal.

Other person who don't care about your presence in a room they hate somewhere and as much early you know this it's that good for you. Being surrounded by all those people who understand you and value your presence also makes a positive impact on your personality.

Initially it's common for people to hide their true side/original and show their calm, entertaining side just to make a proper impression this practice is mostly done in professional fields as it's really important for them to maintain impression and carry their work in a proper flow.

Boys often fake their personality when talking to a girl for the first time, mainly to create a good impression. Their initial goal is to build a positive environment, make a favorable impression, and establish trust. Once these goals are achieved, the real process of getting to know each other begins.

Knowing others is not about quick judgment or surface impressions it is about learning to read the fine interplay between outer behavior and inner identity. Every person carries two sides: The one they show to the world and the one they guard within. The outer person is shaped by manners, tone, and visible actions, but beneath that lies the inner person, whose thoughts and emotions often remain hidden. To truly know someone, you must learn to observe carefully, interpret patiently, and balance empathy with awareness Observation is the first step. Watch how people respond in different contexts how they treat boundaries, how they handle stress, how they behave when no reward is at stake. A single act may mislead, but repeated actions form a pattern. Patterns reveal character more than words. Someone who consistently uplifts others shows genuine kindness. Someone who repeatedly crosses limits shows disregard.

1) Empathy is the second step. Without empathy, observation becomes judgment. A quiet person may be mistaken for arrogant, when in truth they are simply introverted. A talkative person may be seen as shallow, when they may be deeply caring. Empathy allows you to interpret behavior with compassion, to ask: *Why might this person act this way? What story lies behind this action?* It reminds you that every behavior carries a hidden context. Boundaries are the clearest test of character. How someone respects or disrespects boundaries consistently shows their maturity and emotional intelligence. A joke within limits can bond, but a joke that crosses limits can wound. In moments of intensity, filters collapse and honesty spills out. This is the paradox of emotion: the stronger the feeling, the more authentic the words. Observing how people behave in anger or in humor gives your insight into their inner person.
2) Trust is the third dimension. People often present a polished version of themselves in professional or social settings, but their authentic self emerges only in trusted spaces. To know someone deeply, you must earn that trust. Once trust is established, masks fall away, and the inner person reveals itself sometimes vibrant, sometimes vulnerable, always more real than the outer person holds a fake image.

Knowing others also requires patience because identity is not revealed in a single meeting or a single conversation. It unfolds over time, through repeated interactions, through shared experiences, through moments of both joy and difficulty. The outer person may impress you at first, but the inner person will define whether the relationship endures.

Finally, knowing others is about choice. You cannot control how people behave, but you can choose whom to surround yourself with. Surround yourself with those who respect, uplift, and value you. Distance yourself from those who drain, manipulate, or disregard you. This choice shapes your own personality, because the people around you influence your energy, your confidence, and your growth.

How to know other person's inner side?

You can't directly know someone's inner side as if by magic just by looking at them and immediately understanding what type of person they are. In fact, there are only indirect ways to discover someone's inner side, and that happens through one skill observation. Observation is the only way to understand another person, but it has many subtypes, such as noticing their small behaviors, how they act in public and private, how they use their power, their choices, and how they create and maintain boundaries. All of this gives a clear perspective of a person. In reality, if we go deeper there are many more ways, but that increases complexity, so let's keep it simple for now.

When traveling or working in new places, it is important to understand people's behavior for both safety and benefit, to know who falls into the good-to-perfect category for you. Organize people and sort out when you will need a particular person, it truly matters to be with those who take you forward instead of pulling you back.

Chair theory, One of the famous chair theories can directly show you who is there for you and who wants you. Imagine you are invited to an event where people are sitting in a room gossiping, and it's your time to enter. Here, observation reveals possibilities. As soon as you enter, everyone looks at you, and let's say almost every seat is occupied. The person who pulls a seat beside them for you is the one who wants you by their side. Now, if there is only one seat left and the person beside it doesn't call you, it's a clear sign that individual doesn't want you.

Most importantly, if you enter and no one pulls a seat for you, leaving you standing while they continue gossiping, it's a clear sign to leave. No one in the room is interested in you, and if you stay, they will surely ignore you. Self-respect must always be your first and top priority. Look at the power of observation it gives you a clear view of where you belong and where you don't. Some people change their colors like chameleons, showing one personality in public and another in private. Interestingly, that's not always bad. This flips the topic when we talk about the inner side of ourselves.

In every field, someone rules at the top and is unstoppable, and in mastering the inner side, the person who changes personality is often the one ruling. If you face such a person as a competitor, it won't be easy. But if you meet them as a friend, your environment becomes easier, as your inner side may mirror their personality or adopt some of their traits. Others will find it difficult to guess you and that's the point.

Identifying another person's inner side is one of the most complex skills in human interaction. The outer side is visible through appearance, speech, and surface behavior, but the inner side is hidden beneath layers of personality, values, and intentions. You cannot simply look at someone and know their inner world instead, you must rely on careful observation, patience, and interpretation of subtle cues. Observation is the master key, but it is not just about watching it is about noticing patterns, consistency, and contradictions. For example, pay attention to how someone behaves in public versus private, because many wear masks socially but reveal their true nature when they feel safe. Notice how they treat those who cannot benefit them waiters, juniors, or strangers because kindness or arrogance in such moments often reflects true character. Observe their choices what they prioritize, how they spend time, and where they invest energy. Boundaries are another strong indicator those who respect their own and others boundaries usually have clarity and discipline within.

1) Power is also revealing how someone uses authority, whether to uplift or dominate, shows the foundation of their values.
2) Another way to read the inner side is consistency does the person act the same across contexts, or do they change colors like a chameleon? Adaptability can be a strength, but if someone constantly shifts personality to manipulate situations, it may signal cunning rather than authenticity. At the same time, those who adapt sincerely often become powerful allies, because their flexibility teaches resilience.
3) To go deeper, listen not just to words but to silences what someone avoids saying often reveals more than what they speak.
4) Watch their reactions under stress, because pressure strips away masks and shows the raw inner side. Notice long-

term patterns do they keep promises, follow through, and stand firm when values are tested? These are the true mirrors of the inner self.

Ultimately, identifying another person's inner side is not about judgment but clarity. It is about organizing people in your mind knowing who uplifts you, who drains you, and who remains neutral. This clarity helps you decide whom to keep close and whom to keep at a distance, because your environment shapes your growth. The sharper your observation, the more you see beyond appearances into deeper currents of personality. And just as you observe others, remember they observe you too your actions, boundaries, and choices constantly broadcast your own inner side. Mastering this awareness makes you not only a better reader of people but also a stronger guardian of your identity. In the end, the inner side of a person is revealed not in grand gestures but in small, consistent behaviors, and the skill of observation turns those fragments into a clear picture of who they truly are.

INTROVERT

Readers, from this chapter onward the next seven chapters are woven together in a continuous flow. If you are reading this, you are now standing at the center heart of the book the section that will guide you toward discovering the "someone within you." These topics are again repeated in different way in 3rd chapter.

The one person who is mostly silent but when you be his/her life's close person you will understand the person is not actually silent which we call as introvert and that's all because the person hides inner true side. Everyone must have someone their friends or family member who is introvert doesn't talk much in public but in some cases like close friends or in front of love or favorite person they become extrovert, that's all because of comfort and trust they get while being with them. It's natural behavior so it's difficult to change but it's a good example to explain how people change their personality and to give an overall view of two different side. Person have a another person inside which we are calling as inner person but this inner person is a total different person living in a person so you can't judge or just predict the inner person by knowing the outer person.

EVERY EXTROVERT CAN'T HAVE A INTROVERT SIDE BUT EVERY INTROVERT HAS A EXTROVERT SIDE.

Look how people have different visions of an introvert, seeing them as shy, calm, or quiet. But that is their nature, because they choose calmness and peace over chaos and noise. It is a form of energy for them that provides comfort and a way of living where everything is according to their expectations. Have you ever observed how introverts love nature? That is the only place where they forget all the tension they face in everyday life. What nature provides them is all they want a peaceful life. Who doesn't want that? People will say it is the basic need of every person, since everyone is working for that life. But here is where the difference lies, introverts are already living the life others are working to experience. That is where people differ in their inner person, because everyone has one, yet everyone is not the same.

An introvert's inner person finds peace in everything they do whether its love, family, or surroundings. What they want is peace, where everyone is happy, with no tension, no fights, and people believing and trusting each other, energy flowing equally, and everything within boundaries. Their internal world exists within boundaries, where their thoughts, ideas, imagination, and decisions come into existence. They do not enjoy small talk but prefer deep conversation, where dialogue flows so steadily that hours pass unnoticed. One topic links to another like an unbreakable thread, never ending.

Introverts are among the greatest over-thinker's you will meet, thinking deeply before speaking because their mind is like a CPU that never stops running in the background even during sleep. When you meet such a person, observe them sitting alone they are not idle, they are thinking. Their mind is always active, which is why many introverts have high metabolism, burning energy even without exercise. You may know friends who wake up fresh in the morning but feel tired by afternoon or evening despite doing little physical work. The reason is that the processes they undergo are not visible in the physical world, but they are constant inside.

We are not going to talk about extroverts, because they can easily be identified in public within minutes, again through observation by noticing their energy, communication patterns, and behavior. Extroverts communicate freely, start conversations with strangers, and use body language calm posture, relaxed tone, steady eye contact that makes others feel like engaging. Their energy waves outward, drawing attention and making them the center of attraction.

Human beings are layered, complex, and often misunderstood, because what we see on the surface rarely tells the full story of what lies within. This is where empathy in observation matters. Without empathy, you risk misjudging, without attention to patterns, you risk being deceived by isolated incidents. The art of truly knowing others begins with observing outer behavior with compassion, while tracing continuity across time.

Empathy lets you feel the human story behind each moment, while patterns reveal enduring tendencies that shape character. Together, they form a lens that prevents both harsh judgment and blind forgiveness, allowing you to see people not as fragments but as whole beings carrying innocence and wisdom, vulnerability and strength.

Consider the introvert, often labeled shy, quiet, or withdrawn. Yet this outer behavior hides a rich inner world filled with imagination, reflection, and depth. Observe them with empathy and you realize their silence is not emptiness but fullness contained within. Trace their patterns over time and you see they consistently seek peace, meaningful conversations, and environments that nourish rather than drain. Introverts recharge in solitude and expend energy in social chaos. This explains why they appear calm in public yet vibrant in trusted company, why they avoid small talk yet thrive in deep dialogue that flows endlessly like an unbreakable thread. Their inner person is alive, layered, and waiting to be discovered but only by those who earn their trust. Trust is the gateway that unlocks their extroverted side, revealing humor, warmth, and even leadership. This duality shows that every introvert carries an extrovert within, though not every extrovert carries an introvert inside. And this difference highlights the uniqueness of inner persons across individuals. We will see duality in detail in next topic.

The hidden inner person plays a profound role in shaping identity, because every individual carries a side that is not visible to the public, a side that emerges only in trusted company or unguarded moments, and this inner person is often different from the outer mask. People may present a polished version of themselves in professional or romantic settings, but their authentic self emerges in moments of stress, intimacy, or vulnerability, and the gap between the performed self and the authentic self is where true understanding lies. Empathy allows us to respect this gap, while patterns allow us to measure whether the performed self-aligns with the authentic self over time, and together they reveal the truth of character.

Introverts, in particular, embody the richness of the inner person, because their silence hides constant mental activity, their overthinking reflects deep processing, and their preference for nature shows their desire for peace, they may appear tired even without physical exertion because their mind is always active, burning energy invisibly, and this inner process explains why they often carry creativity, empathy, and insight. Their inner person seeks harmony, trust, and meaningful connection, and when you observe them with empathy and trace their patterns, you realize their quietness is not weakness but strength, a way of protecting the richness within.

Extroverts, on the other hand, show their energy outwardly, but even here the inner person matters, because their charisma may be genuine or performative, their confidence may be rooted in stability or in the need for validation, and only by combining empathy with patterns can we discern the difference their outer behavior may attract attention, but their inner person reveals whether they truly value others or simply seek to dominate, and this distinction is essential in knowing them fully.

So when you look at someone whether introvert or extrovert, silent or expressive, calm or angry don't stop at the surface but they step back to see the patterns and feel the moment, the ability to see people not as fragments but as whole beings, carrying both their struggles and their strengths, both their innocence and their wisdom, both their outer mask and their inner person and this is the essence of human connection, the foundation of respect, and the path to living a life that honors both the child within and the elder you are destined to become.

The Inner Sanctuary of Silence

Silence is often mistaken for emptiness. To many, it feels like a void that must be filled with words, music, or by spending time with someone or in nature. But for the introvert, silence is not absence it is presence. It is the sanctuary where the "someone within you" awakens. In silence, the introvert listens not just to the world, but to themselves, to inner-self giving time to self and at particular moment introvert are in deep state communicating with inner-self just like meditation a person deep inside in thoughts, if someone tries to break their concentration some introverts may get angry as they lost the focus and thc conncction arc broken. Every heartbeat, every breath, every subtle vibration of life becomes audible minor change in surrounding are also noticed just a hyper sensitive sensor. Silence is not passive, it is active awareness. It is the moment when the mind stops reacting to the outside and begins reflecting on the inside.

This is why introverts appear calm. Their silence is not a lack of thought but it's like a abundant source for introvert where imagination paints, where memory sketches, where philosophy writes itself. Extroverts may thrive in the noise of crowds, but introverts thrive in the quiet of solitude. Silence is also a shield. It protects the inner person from chaos, from judgment, from unnecessary exposure. Within silence, the introvert builds strength, clarity, and resilience. It is here that they prepare for the world, not by rehearsing words but by aligning their spirit.

The sanctuary of silence is not loneliness. It is companionship with oneself. It is the realization that peace is not found outside but cultivated inside by yourself and inner-self. For the introvert, silence is not only a silence, it's worth more than silence. Something which creates

Silence also sharpens perception. When noise is removed, the smallest details become visible: the way light falls on a wall, the rhythm of footsteps, the subtle emotions in a friend's voice. Introverts notice these details because silence trains them to observe. Their inner person thrives on such awareness, turning ordinary moments into profound realizations. This sanctuary is also creative. Many introverts produce their best work in silence writing, painting, composing, or simply imagining. Silence is the soil where ideas germinate. It is the womb of creation, where the inner person gives birth to thoughts that later shape the outer world.

But silence is not always easy. In a society that equates noise with success, silence is often misunderstood as weakness. Introverts must learn to defend their sanctuary, to explain that silence is not avoidance but alignment. It is not rejection but reflection. It is not emptiness but fullness. The "someone within you" thrives in silence because silence is truth. It strips away masks, distractions, and pretenses. It reveals the raw essence of who you are. And for the introvert, that essence is not something to be shouted it is something to be lived.

Explaining the concept of "someone within you" to an introvert is effortless, as they already live in constant companionship with their inner self. Silence is not unfamiliar to them it is a natural state they can embrace for an entire day without discomfort. This ability is unique, impossible to replicate, and far from easy. In contrast, extroverts often struggle when left alone. Within hours, frustration sets in, prompting them to seek tasks or reach out to others to fill the void. Observers may commend extroverts for finding work or companionship, and indeed, that is a constructive choice. Yet, from another perspective, the same extrovert lacks the capacity to remain steady in solitude, a strength that introverts embody with ease. The art of dedicating time to oneself and engaging in deep communication with the inner self is a gift reserved for introverts. They can access it at any moment, in any place. Interestingly, those who excel at multitasking are often introverts, for this ability stems from their natural inclination to balance inner dialogue with external action.

Silence, when seen through the lens of the inner person, is not simply the absence of sound but the presence of awareness, a sanctuary where introverts discover their deepest truths and nurture their hidden strength. What often remains unexplored is how silence becomes a **multi-layered resource** a shield, a teacher, a creative soil, and a mirror of identity. For introverts, silence is not passive it is active engagement with the inner self. It is the moment when the outer noise dissolves and the

Silence also acts as a **teacher**. It sharpens perception, training introverts to notice details others overlook the way light shifts across a wall, the rhythm of footsteps, the subtle emotions in a friend's voice. This heightened awareness is not accidental it is cultivated by silence. Introverts learn to observe deeply, to listen beyond words, to sense the unspoken. Their inner person thrives on such awareness, turning ordinary moments into profound realizations. In this way, silence teaches patience, attentiveness, and empathy.

At the same time, silence is a **creative soil**. Many introverts produce their best work in solitude writing, painting, composing, or imagining. Silence is the womb of creation, where ideas germinate and grow into visions that later shape the outer world. The inner person uses silence as a canvas, painting with imagination, sketching with memory, writing with philosophy. This is why introverts often excel in creative pursuits their silence is not emptiness but abundance, a reservoir of ideas waiting to be expressed.

Silence is also a **mirror of identity**. It reflects the duality between the outer person and the inner person. Extroverts may thrive in crowds, drawing energy from noise and interaction, but introverts thrive in solitude, drawing energy from reflection and imagination. This difference is not weakness but uniqueness. Silence allows introverts to live in companionship with themselves, to cultivate peace inside rather than chase it outside. It is a realization that fulfillment is not found in external validation but in internal harmony.

Yet silence is not always easy. In a society that equates noise with productivity, silence is often misunderstood as weakness. Introverts must learn to defend their sanctuary, to explain that silence is not emptiness but fullness, not avoidance but alignment. They must remind themselves that silence is a gift, a strength, a source of clarity. The "Someone Within You" thrives in silence because silence is the language of authenticity. It is where the inner person speaks most clearly, guiding you toward self-belief and resilience.

Ultimately, the inner sanctuary of silence is where the "Someone Within You" awakens. It is where imagination paints, memory sketches, philosophy writes itself. It is where the inner person listens, guides, and restores. Silence is not emptiness it is presence. It is not loneliness it is companionship with oneself. It is not weakness it is strength. For introverts, silence is the ultimate sanctuary, the place where they align with their inner person, preserve their energy, and prepare to face the world with authenticity.

The Duality of Energy

Introverts live with a paradox. They appear reserved, yet inside they hold oceans of energy. This energy is not scattered outward but concentrated inward. Unlike extroverts, who recharge through social interaction, introverts recharge through solitude, reflection, and meaningful connection. Energy for an introvert is sacred.

They do not waste it on small talk or superficial encounters. Instead, they invest it in people who matter, in conversations that transform, and in pursuits that align with their values. This is why introverts often seem selective because they are. Their energy is finite, and they guard it like treasure.

The "Someone Within You" is this hidden reservoir of energy. It is the part of the introvert that bursts forth when trust is established. Suddenly, the quiet person becomes animated, expressive, and even extroverted but only in safe spaces. This duality is not contradiction it is balance. The outer calm protects the inner fire. This duality also explains why introverts often feel drained after social events. Their energy is not limitless, it is carefully rationed. They give deeply, but only to those who matter. And when they withdraw, it is not rejection it is restoration.

Energy for introverts is like currency. Every interaction is a transaction, and they spend carefully. A meaningless conversation may cost more than it gives, while a deep dialogue may feel like an investment that multiplies. This is why introverts often prefer fewer but richer connections. The duality of energy also manifests in creativity. Introverts may appear quiet, but their inner person is bursting with ideas, visions, and dreams. When they channel this energy into art, writing, or innovation, the results are profound. Their silence hides a storm, and when the storm is released, it transforms everything around them. But this duality requires balance. Too much outward energy can lead to exhaustion too much inward energy can lead to isolation. The introvert must learn to navigate both worlds, to honor their need for solitude while embracing their capacity for connection.

The "Someone Within You" is the guardian of this balance. It knows when to speak and when to stay silent, when to give and when to withdraw, when to shine and when to rest. It is the inner compass that guides the introvert through the paradox of energy. This duality is not weakness it is strength. It allows introverts to live in two worlds: the outer world of calm and the inner world of fire. It is proof that silence does not mean emptiness, and solitude does not mean loneliness. It means the energy is being preserved for what truly matters. If you see introvert who is quite, calm, silent it doesn't mean the person is different from the world, the only thing which makes both different is presence of mind and mentality to understand our-self (inner-self).

The duality of nature in identifying someone within you is total different, where one lives for himself mostly and another lives in the present moment only. You might see introvert calm but they live for themselves and they enjoy their company with the nature as if one boss trying to give credit to his team member where members are our inner personalities and extrovert are like hikers full on vibe climbing the tough mountain, giving their best to see the beautiful view from the top after giving 100% in the way.

The duality of energy in introverts is not just about how they manage their social presence, but about how they live in two worlds simultaneously the outer world of calm and the inner world of fire. What often goes missing in discussions of this paradox is the emotional intelligence and self-awareness that introverts cultivate through this balance. Their energy is not scattered outward but concentrated inward, and this inward concentration allows them to observe, reflect, and understand themselves and others at a deeper level. Unlike extroverts, who thrive on external stimulation, introverts thrive on internal alignment. They measure their interactions not by quantity but by quality, and this selectivity is not arrogance but wisdom.

Relationship between energy and identity. Energy is not just fuel for action it is the essence of how a person defines themselves. For introverts, energy is sacred because it is tied to authenticity. They do not waste it on superficial encounters because such encounters do not resonate with their inner person. Instead, they invest it in people who matter, in conversations that transform, and in pursuits that align with their values. This is why introverts often appear reserved in public but become vibrant in trusted spaces their energy is not gone, it is preserved, waiting for the right moment to be released.

Another dimension is the impact of energy on creativity and productivity. Introverts may seem quiet, but their inner person is bursting with ideas, visions, and dreams. Their silence hides storms of thought, and when those storms are channeled into writing, art, or innovation, the results are profound. This is why many introverts excel in creative fields they use their concentrated energy to build worlds within themselves and then share those worlds with others. Their duality of energy allows them to balance solitude with expression, reflection with creation.

The duality also extends to relationships and trust. Introverts give deeply, but only to those who matter. Their energy is finite, and they guard it like treasure. When they withdraw, it is not rejection it is restoration. This withdrawal is often misunderstood by others as disinterest, but in reality, it is a necessary act of self-preservation. Introverts know that to give authentically, they must first recharge. Their inner person acts as a guardian, guiding them when to speak and when to stay silent, when to give and when to withdraw, when to shine and when to rest.

The duality of energy also reveals the contrast between introverts and extroverts. Extroverts are like hikers climbing a mountain with full energy, giving their best to see the beautiful view from the top, thriving on the collective vibe of the climb. Introverts, on the other hand, are like the mountain itself silent, steady, and full of hidden strength. They live for themselves, enjoying their own company, and their inner personalities are like team members working together quietly to sustain balance. This difference does not make one better than the other, it simply shows that energy manifests differently depending on the inner person.

What is often overlooked is the role of nature in this duality. In next topic we will look how nature acts as mirror showing one individual inner side. Introverts find peace in natural surroundings because nature mirrors their inner world calm on the surface, yet full of hidden energy beneath. Just as rivers flow quietly but carry immense power, introverts live calmly but hold oceans of energy within. Nature provides them with the environment to recharge, to align their inner person with the outer world, and to remind them that solitude is not loneliness but restoration.

Finally, the missing piece is the lesson this duality teaches us about self-understanding. The presence of mind and mentality to understand oneself is what sets introverts apart. They know that energy is not limitless, and they respect its boundaries. They understand that solitude is not isolation but a way of reconnecting with the inner person. They realize that silence is not emptiness but preservation. And they embrace the paradox that they can be both calm and fiery, both reserved and expressive, both solitary and connected.

Nature as the mirror of the Inner Person

For introverts, nature is not just scenery it is a mirror. The rustling of leaves, the flow of rivers, the stillness of mountains all reflect their inner world. Where society demands performance, nature offers presence. Where people demand words, nature offers silence. Walking through a forest, the introvert does not feel alone. They feel accompanied by something greater, something that understands without asking. The quiet of the forest mirrors their own quiet. The endless sky mirrors their imagination. The steady rhythm of waves mirrors their thought process. This connection is not accidental. Introverts thrive in environments where peace is natural, not forced. Nature does not judge, does not interrupt, and does not demand. It simply exists. And in that existence, the introvert finds belonging. The "Someone Within You" thrives in such spaces, because nature validates their choice of peace over chaos.

Nature also teaches boundaries. A tree grows within its roots, a river flows within its banks, a mountain stands within its limits. Introverts, too, live within boundaries not as restrictions but as definitions of self. Their inner person flourishes when life is structured, when peace is protected, when chaos is kept at bay. But nature is not only peace it is also power. Storms, winds, and floods remind the introvert that silence does not mean weakness. Stillness can hold immense strength. This duality resonates deeply: the quiet person may appear calm, but inside they hold storms of thought, oceans of imagination, and mountains of resilience. For the introvert, nature is philosophy. It is proof that silence is powerful, that stillness is alive, that peace is not weakness but wisdom. The "Someone Within You" finds in nature a reflection of its own truth: that life is not about noise, but about harmony.

Nature as the mirror of the inner person is not only a poetic idea it is a lived truth for those who seek meaning in silence.

For introverts, the forest, the river, the mountain, and the sky are not external landscapes but internal reflections. They walk into nature and discover themselves. The rustling of leaves is not noise, it is dialogue. The stillness of mountains is not emptiness, it is presence. The endless sky is not distance, it is imagination. In these spaces, the introvert feels understood without explanation, accompanied without conversation, and validated without judgment.

This connection is profound because society often demands performance constant words, constant action, and constant proof of worth. Nature demands nothing. It simply exists, and in that existence, it teaches the introvert that being is enough. The "Someone Within You" thrives here, because peace is not forced, it is natural. Silence is not awkward, it is alive. Stillness is not weakness, it is wisdom.

Boundaries are another lesson nature offers. A tree grows only within the reach of its roots, a river flows only within its banks, a mountain stands only within its limits. These boundaries are not restrictions, they are definitions. They give shape, identity, and strength. Introverts, too, flourish when their boundaries are respected. They protect their energy, they choose their spaces, and they define their limits. And just as nature's boundaries create harmony, so do theirs. Without boundaries, chaos invades, with boundaries, peace is preserved.

Yet nature is not only gentle it is powerful. Storms, winds, floods, and earthquakes remind us that silence can hold immense strength. This duality resonates deeply with the introvert. Outwardly calm, inwardly vast. Outwardly quiet, inwardly storming with thought. Outwardly still, inwardly alive with imagination. The introvert sees in nature a philosophy: silence is not emptiness, it is fullness. Stillness is not weakness, it is resilience. Peace is not escape, it is wisdom.

This is why the inner person finds belonging in nature. The "Someone Within You" recognizes itself in the rhythm of waves, the patience of trees, and the permanence of mountains. It learns that life is not about noise but about harmony. It learns that boundaries are not cages but sanctuaries. It learns that silence is not absence but presence. And most importantly, it learns that the real strength of a person lies not in how loudly they speak, but in how deeply they live.

For the introvert, nature is not scenery it is scripture. It teaches without words, it guides without commands, it heals without effort. It shows that the path to authenticity is not through performance but through presence. The inner person, when mirrored in nature, discovers its own truth: that peace is not a luxury, it is a necessity, that silence is not isolation, it is connection, that boundaries are not barriers, they are definitions of self.

And so, when you walk into a forest, sit by a river, or gaze at the sky, remembers you are not looking at something outside of you. You are looking at yourself. Nature is the mirror, and the reflection is your inner person. The "Someone Within You" thrives here, because here, you are reminded that life's deepest wisdom is not found in noise, but in harmony.

Meditation

Nature has always been the most honest mirror of the inner person, and meditation is the practice that allows us to look into that mirror with clarity. When you sit in silence, away from distractions, and allow yourself to breathe in rhythm with the natural world, you begin to communicate with the deeper layers of your being. Meditation is not about escaping reality. It is about aligning with it. Just as rivers flow steadily, mountains stand strong, and trees grow patiently, meditation teaches you to embody these qualities within yourself. By observing nature during meditation whether it is the sound of wind, the stillness of water, or the warmth of sunlight, you begin to recognize similar currents inside your mind and soul. This recognition is the first step in understanding your inner person and understanding yourself.

Meditation benefits communication with the inner self because it quiets the noise of the outer world or eliminates unwanted distraction from our living surrounding. In daily life, we are constantly bombarded with opinions, judgments, and expectations, which cloud our perception of who we truly are. But when you meditate, you strip away those layers and allow your authentic voice to emerge inside you. It is like polishing a mirror until it reflects a clear image of you. You begin to notice your thoughts without being controlled by them, and this awareness shows you the patterns of your inner side your fears, your strengths, your desires, and your values. Over time, meditation strengthens discipline and clarity, making your inner foundation unshakable.

Another benefit is emotional balance. Just as nature maintains harmony between seasons, meditation helps you balance the seasons of your mind. Anger, sadness, joy, and peace all flow through you, but meditation teaches you not to resist or cling to them. Instead, you observe them as passing clouds, realizing that your inner person is deeper than temporary emotions. This balance allows you to interact with others more authentically, because when you know your own inner side, you can better understand theirs.

Meditation also enhances the soft voice of the inner person that often gets drowned out by external noise. In silence, intuition becomes louder, guiding you toward decisions that align with your true self. It is like listening to the whispers of the forest or the rhythm of the ocean, the more you tune in, the more you understand the language of your inner being. Ultimately, meditation is the bridge between nature and the inner person. It teaches you patience like a tree, resilience like a mountain, and flow like a river. By practicing it regularly, you create a dialogue with your inner side, discovering not only who you are but also how you can grow. In this way, meditation becomes more than a practice it becomes a mirror, reflecting your deepest self and helping you walk the path of clarity, discipline, and self-respect.

Dear Reader,

Talking with yourself is the most honest dialogue you can ever have, and meditation in nature is the doorway to that conversation. When you sit in silence, breathing with awareness, you begin to hear the subtle voice of your inner self. The one often hidden beneath noise and distractions, discovering your values, strengths, and clarity. In 3rd chapter of this book, ''Talk with Yourself'' we are going to continue in meditation topic, how can one use meditation to communicate with inner-self i.e. "Someone Within You" which makes meditation your daily way to message yourself, a moment where you listen to yourself and connect with the person within who guides your growth and shapes your destiny.

The Overthinking Mind

To call introverts "over-thinker" is both accurate and incomplete. Their mind is not just overthinking it is over-processing, overanalyzing, over-imagining. Like a CPU running in the background, their thoughts never stop. Even in sleep, their subconscious continues to weave scenarios, solutions, and reflections. This constant mental activity explains why introverts often feel drained without physical exertion. Their energy is consumed by invisible labor analyzing conversations, replaying decisions, imagining outcomes. While extroverts expend energy outward, introverts expend it inward.

But this overthinking is also their gift. It makes them empathetic, cautious, and wise. They rarely speak without thought, and when they do, their words carry weight. The "Someone Within You" is this hidden engine always running, always processing, always shaping the person's reality. The challenge, however, is balance. Overthinking can become overburdening. The mind that creates wisdom can also create worry. The introvert must learn to channel their thoughts into creation, not destruction. Meditation, writing, art, and nature become tools to transform overthinking into insight. This hidden engine also explains why introverts often excel in problem-solving. They anticipate outcomes, consider consequences, and prepare for possibilities others overlook. Their mind is not just thinking it is rehearsing life. And while this can be exhausting, it also makes them resilient.

The "Someone Within You" thrives in this mental depth. It is the part of the introvert that sees connections others miss, that imagines futures others cannot, that feels emotions others ignore. Overthinking is not a flaw it is a feature. It is the hidden power that turns silence into wisdom.

Overthinking for an introvert is not just a mental loop it is a conversation with the inner self. When thoughts begin to spiral, the introvert doesn't merely observe them, they step into the moment completely, as if entering a private dialogue. Every possibility, every doubt, every memory is examined with care. This process can feel heavy, but it also reveals the depth of their inner world. The "Someone Within You" is present in these moments, listening patiently, guiding silently, and reminding you that not every thought deserves your energy. It is as if the inner person becomes both the questioner and the answerer, holding space for reflection until clarity emerges. Later in book we will talk on inner-self where I will pitch whole idea of Someone Within You.

The way introverts talk with their inner self during overthinking is subtle yet profound. They may not speak aloud, but inside, there is a rhythm of dialogue questions asked, answers weighed, emotions acknowledged. They are fully immersed, almost unaware of the outside world, because their attention is drawn inward. This is why introverts often appear lost in thought, they are not absent, and they are deeply present with themselves. In those moments, they are exploring the layers of their mind, searching for meaning, and negotiating with their own emotions. It is a process of being totally in the moment, where silence becomes the language of self-communication.

Yet, this inward dialogue is both a gift and a challenge. Overthinking can drain energy when the mind circles endlessly without resolution. But it can also sharpen awareness, uncover insights, and lead to creativity. The inner person acts like a compass, helping to separate noise from truth. When listened to carefully, it shows which thoughts are worth keeping and which can be released. This is why introverts often emerge from solitude with new ideas, fresh perspectives, or creative breakthroughs. Their overthinking, when guided by the inner self, transforms chaos into clarity.

The paradox is that overthinking feels like a storm, but within that storm lies wisdom. The inner person knows when to pause, when to redirect, and when to rest. It teaches the introvert that silence is not emptiness, but a space where energy is preserved for what truly matters. Overthinking, then, is not weakness it is a pathway to understanding, provided the inner dialogue is honored. The introvert learns to balance thought and stillness, to guard their energy, and to trust the quiet voice within.

Overthinking is not just a mental loop it is a lens through which introverts experience the world. Every detail, every word, every gesture is processed with intensity. This makes them highly sensitive to nuance, often noticing what others overlook. They replay conversations not to torture themselves, but to understand meaning, tone, and intent. This heightened awareness can make them empathetic, because they imagine how others feel, and cautious, because they anticipate consequences before acting. Yet it can also make them vulnerable, because the same sensitivity that gives them insight can also magnify hurt.

Relationship between overthinking and emotional depth. Introverts don't just analyze facts they analyze feelings. They reflect on how their words might have affected someone, how their decisions might ripple outward, how their presence might be perceived. This emotional processing is why they often appear reserved they are not indifferent, they are deeply considerate. Their inner person acts as a mirror, showing them not only what they did but how it might have been received. This makes them compassionate friends and thoughtful partners, but it also means they carry invisible burdens of worry and self-doubt.

Another layer is the connection between overthinking and creativity. The same mind that spins scenarios also spins ideas. Introverts often excel in writing, art, or innovation because their inner dialogue transforms into expression. What feels like endless thought becomes fuel for imagination. Their overthinking is not wasted energy it is raw material for creation. When guided by the inner person, their thoughts become stories, philosophies, or solutions. This is why solitude often produces breakthroughs their mind, left uninterrupted, organizes chaos into clarity.

Overthinking also plays a role in resilience and preparation. Introverts rehearse life in their minds. They anticipate outcomes, consider consequences, and prepare for possibilities others overlook. This mental rehearsal makes them resilient in crises, because they have already imagined the scenarios. They may appear cautious, but their caution is strength it is foresight. The inner person acts like a strategist, guiding them through uncertainty with plans already formed in silence.

Yet the challenge remains: balance. Overthinking can become overburdening when thoughts spiral without resolution. The missing piece is the practice of transforming thought into stillness. Meditation, writing, art, and nature are not hobbies for introverts they are survival tools. They allow the mind to release excess energy, to transform worry into wisdom, to turn loops into lines of clarity. The inner person knows when to pause, when to redirect, and when to rest. It teaches that not every thought deserves energy, and that silence is not emptiness but preservation.

Finally, overthinking reveals the dialogue between outer and inner identity. Outwardly, introverts may appear quiet, but inwardly they are in constant conversation with themselves. This dialogue is subtle yet profound: questions asked, answers weighed, emotions acknowledged. It is a rhythm of self-communication, where the inner person becomes both questioner and answerer. This is why introverts often appear lost in thought they are not absent, they are deeply present with themselves. And this presence, though invisible, is their greatest strength.

Deep Conversation

Introverts dislike small talk not because they are antisocial, but because they crave depth. A shallow exchange feels like wasted energy, while a deep conversation feels like nourishment. When an introvert finds someone who can dive into topics of meaning philosophy, dreams, fears, love their inner person awakens. Such conversations are not linear. They flow like rivers, branching into tributaries, connecting one idea to another. Hours pass unnoticed because the dialogue is not just words it is soul meeting soul. This is the introvert's true extroversion: not in crowds, but in intimacy.

The "Someone Within You" thrives in these moments. It is the part of the introvert that longs for connection beyond surface, beyond masks, beyond performance. It is the part that believes communication should be a bridge, not a transaction. Deep conversations also reveal trust. Introverts do not open easily, but when they do, it is a gift. They share not just facts but feelings, not just opinions but truths. And in return, they expect the same honesty. This is why introverts often form fewer but stronger bonds their connections are built on depth, not breadth.

These conversations are also creative. They spark ideas, inspire visions, and build philosophies. For introverts, dialogue is not just communication it is collaboration of minds. The "someone within you" finds in these threads the unbreakable link between self and other, between thought and expression, between silence and speech.

In a world obsessed with speed, deep conversations are timeless. They remind us that connection is not measured in words spoken but in truths shared. For the introvert, this is the ultimate expression of their inner person: not noise, not performance, but meaning.

Deep conversation is one of the most profound expressions of human connection, especially for introverts, because it is not about exchanging words but about exchanging truths, and when we look closely at why introverts crave depth, we begin to understand that their silence in small talk is not rejection of people but rejection of superficiality they dislike shallow exchanges because such interactions feel like wasted energy, while deep conversations feel like nourishment, like food for the soul, and this is why when an introvert finds someone who can dive into topics of meaning philosophy, dreams, fears, love their inner person awakens, revealing a side that is otherwise hidden from the world. These conversations are not linear, they flow like rivers, branching into tributaries, connecting one idea to another, and hours pass unnoticed because the dialogue is not just words but soul meeting soul, and this is the introvert's true extroversion: not in crowds, but in intimacy, not in noise, but in meaning.

The "someone within you" thrives in these moments, because it is the part of the introvert that longs for connection beyond surface, beyond masks, beyond performance, and it is the part that believes communication should be a bridge, not a transaction. Deep conversations reveal trust, because introverts do not open easily, but when they do, it is a gift, they share not just facts but feelings, not just opinions but truths, and in return, they expect the same honesty, which is why introverts often form fewer but stronger bonds their connections are built on depth, not breadth. These conversations are also creative, sparking ideas, inspiring visions, and building philosophies, because for introverts dialogue is not just communication, it is collaboration of minds, and the "someone within you" finds in these threads the unbreakable link between self and other, between thought and expression, between silence and speech.

But what is often missing in our understanding of deep conversation is the psychological and emotional mechanics behind it. For introverts, small talk drains energy because it demands outward performance without inward meaning, while deep conversation replenishes energy because it aligns with their inner values. This is why introverts may appear tired after social gatherings filled with surface chatter, yet feel alive after hours of meaningful dialogue with one trusted person. Their energy is not measured by the number of people they interact with, but by the quality of those interactions. Deep conversation is their form of recharging, their way of aligning the outer world with the inner person.

Another missing dimension is the role of listening. Introverts are often excellent listeners, and deep conversations thrive on listening as much as speaking. In small talk, listening is shallow, often waiting for a chance to reply, but in deep conversation, listening becomes active, empathetic, and transformative. Introverts listen not just to words but to pauses, tones, and emotions, and this attentive listening creates a safe space where the other person feels truly heard. This is why deep conversations with introverts often feel healing they are not rushing to fill silence, they are honoring it, allowing meaning to emerge naturally.

Deep conversation also reveals the inner architecture of trust. Introverts do not open their inner world to everyone, they choose carefully, and once chosen, they invest deeply. This selectivity is not arrogance but protection, because their inner person is precious, and exposing it requires assurance that the other will respect it. Trust, once established, transforms the introvert from silent observer to vibrant participant, and this transformation is not superficial it is the unveiling of their authentic self. In this way, deep conversation is both a test and a gift: a test of whether someone can handle truth, and a gift of revealing the inner person.

We must also understand the creative dimension of deep conversation. For introverts, dialogue is not just about sharing experiences but about co-creating meaning. A conversation about philosophy may spark a new idea, a discussion about dreams may inspire a vision, and a reflection on fears may lead to courage. Deep conversations are fertile grounds for creativity because they allow introverts to externalize their inner thoughts, to weave imagination into dialogue, and to build philosophies in collaboration with others. This is why introverts often excel in writing, art, or innovation their creativity is nurtured by conversations that go beyond the surface.

Finally, deep conversation highlights the contrast between outer and inner behavior. An introvert may appear quiet, reserved, or even distant in public, but in deep conversation they reveal humor, warmth, and passion. This duality shows that outer silence does not equal inner emptiness it equals inner richness waiting for the right context. Deep conversation is the key that unlocks this richness, the bridge between the outer mask and the inner person. And once unlocked, it reveals that introverts are not antisocial but selectively social, not silent but deeply expressive, not distant but profoundly connected.

In conclusion, deep conversation is the ultimate expression of the introvert's inner person. It is where empathy meets trust, where listening meets creativity, where silence meets meaning. It is not noise, not performance, but truth. It is the nourishment that introverts crave, the energy that sustains them, the gift they offer to those who earn their trust.

In a world that often values breadth over depth, speed over presence, performance over authenticity, deep conversations remind us of the timeless truth connection is not about how much we speak, but about how deeply we share. For introverts, this is not just a preference it is a way of living, a philosophy of communication, and a reflection of the inner person who longs not for crowds but for communion, not for attention but for authenticity, not for small talk but for soul talk.

SOMEONE WITHIN YOU

Let's talk about the main topic till now you have got an overall idea what is outer person and what is inner person. A person who is in us but its behavior is different than how we behave in our day to day life. Someone only you know about that person it might be your weakness or it might be your strength but that side should not be exposed to anyone keep that in mind no one literally no one weather the person is you love or your parents or your friends.

This side of you must be preserved because anyone can use it against you if it's your weakness, can you trust 100% on other person? No, even if the inner person is your strength still it's your job to keep it hidden only use it when required do not even try to show off you have a hidden skill or talent which you don't use.

Somewhere or somewhere you are exposing yourself just like a wound which is covered by bandage.

Some people look normal from outside but they are weak from inside emotionally and they don't know how to react when some incident occur with them and due to their such behavior some people take benefit from these type of people. Your inner person is your strength it is your support when no one is with you have yourself and this book is written to find your inner-self. My only motive is to make people aware of the true potential which everyone carry in them instead of searching outside have a look inside you a person is sleeping just wake him up.

Someone Within You will give you just vision to look rest everything is on you reader how you use it, just like showing you path to climb mountain every decision is yours do you have to climb the mountain or not? But if you are reading this book it means you are here to climb the mountain and in all the way if you feel you are alone don't worry you have Someone Within You. All you can do is believe in yourself which is self-believe, trust the person living inside you and do it all for the kid who is still alive in you. You must have seen how grandparents are more close to grandchildren, more friendly you must have also experienced this and that's why grandparents feel like mirrors to the child still alive in us. They don't judge, they don't demand, they simply play, laugh, and listen. That's the same way you must treat the kid within you be gentle, be playful, be curious. Because that kid is the one who reminds you that climbing the mountain is not just about reaching the top, it's about enjoying the climb, the view, the air, the struggle, the joy.

When you walk with Someone Within You, you carry both wisdom and innocence. Wisdom tells you the path, innocence gives you the courage to step on it. And whenever you feel tired, remember how a child never stops asking questions, never stops imagining, never stops believing. That is your fuel.

The journey of discovering *Someone Within You* is not about creating a new identity but about uncovering the one that has always been there, quietly shaping your choices, silently guiding your emotions, and patiently waiting for you to notice. This inner person is not visible to the world, yet it is the most authentic version of you. It is the child who once dreamed without fear, the elder who will one day reflect with wisdom, and the present self who stands at the crossroads of both. To understand this inner person, you must first accept that the outer world often demands masks roles we play, behaviors we adopt, impressions we maintain. But beneath those masks lies the true self, the one who feels deeply, thinks endlessly, and carries both your vulnerabilities and your strengths.

This inner person is your hidden reservoir of energy. When the outer world exhausts you with noise, expectations, and performance, the inner person restores you with silence, imagination, and meaning. It is the part of you that craves peace when chaos surrounds you, that seeks depth when conversations feel shallow, that finds comfort in nature when society feels overwhelming. Introverts embody this truth most visibly, but it exists in everyone. The outer person may laugh in crowds, but the inner person longs for intimacy. The outer person may appear strong, but the inner person may carry wounds. The outer person may seem silent, but the inner person may be overflowing with thoughts.

To preserve this inner person is to protect your essence. Not everything about you must be exposed, because exposure invites judgment, and judgment can distort truth. Your inner person is like a sacred flame if shown recklessly, it can be blown out by others, if guarded wisely, and it can light your path when darkness surrounds you. This is why trust becomes the gateway. You cannot trust 100% on anyone, not even those closest to you, because every human carries their own limitations. But you can trust *Someone Within You*, because that person is you. That is your ultimate support system, the voice that whispers courage when fear rises, the strength that holds you when loneliness strikes, and the wisdom that guides you when confusion clouds your mind.

Think of the mountain metaphor: life is the climb, and the inner person is your companion. The outer world may cheer you when you start, may doubt you when you stumble, may ignore you when you pause. But the inner person never leaves. It reminds you that climbing is not just about reaching the summit it is about enjoying the air, the view, the struggle, the joy. The child within you brings curiosity to the climb, asking questions, imagining possibilities, believing in magic. The elder within you brings wisdom, reminding you of patience, resilience, and perspective. Together, they form the balance of innocence and maturity, courage and caution, dream and discipline.

When you walk with *Someone Within You*, you carry both sides of time the past and the future woven into your present. The child reminds you to play, to laugh, to wonder. The elder reminds you to reflect, to endure, to grow. And in moments of fatigue, when the climb feels endless, remember how a child never stops asking questions, never stops imagining, never stops believing. That is your fuel. Remember how an elder never stops teaching, never stops guiding, never stops reminding you of the bigger picture. That is your compass.

Deep conversations are one of the ways the inner person awakens. Introverts dislike small talk not because they are antisocial, but because they crave depth. A shallow exchange feels like wasted energy, while a deep conversation feels like nourishment. When the inner person finds someone who can dive into topics of meaning philosophy, dreams, fears, love it comes alive. Such conversations are not linear, they flow like rivers, branching into tributaries, connecting one idea to another. Hours pass unnoticed because the dialogue is not just words it is soul meeting soul. This is the introvert's true extroversion not in crowds, but in intimacy. And this is the inner person's true joy: not in performance, but in authenticity.

The inner person thrives in trust. It does not open easily, but when it does, it shares not just facts but feelings, not just opinions but truths. And in return, it expects honesty. This is why introverts often form fewer but stronger bonds their connections are built on depth, not breadth. The inner person values quality over quantity, meaning over appearance, truth over transaction. And when such bonds are formed, they become unbreakable threads, linking self to other, thought to expression, and silence to speech.

Creativity also flows from the inner person. Dialogue becomes collaboration of minds, sparking ideas, inspiring visions, building philosophies. The inner person is not passive, it is active, alive, and endlessly imaginative. It is the part of you that writes, paints, and dreams, invents, and creates. It is the part that sees beyond what is and imagines what could be. And when you nurture it, you discover that your greatest strength lies not in what the world sees, but in what you carry within.

In a world obsessed with speed, performance, and appearances, the inner person reminds you of timeless truths. Connection is not measured in words spoken but in truths shared. Success is not measured in applause but in authenticity. Strength is not measured in noise but in resilience. The outer person may chase recognition, but the inner person seeks meaning. The outer person may fear judgment, but the inner person knows self-belief. The outer person may feel alone, but the inner person whispers: *you are never alone, because you have me.*

So preserve this inner person. Guard it like a treasure, nurture it like a child, and respect it like an elder. Use it when required, but never flaunt it. Let it be your hidden strength, your silent companion, your ultimate truth. Because when the world doubts you, when people misunderstand you, when loneliness surrounds you, *Someone Within You* will remain. And that is enough.

LOVE

To all lovers this topic is for you, have you ever observed your-self how your behavior and character change when you are talking, texting or spending time with that one person you love. You switch your-self from one person to another inside for love you're a total different person at the present moment which I call it as character switch, don't confuse between character of person here for now character means a person who is playing a role.
According to science this switch happens because of biochemical and psychological state. Human brain releases hormone which are associated to love such as Oxytocin which is bonding hormone, Dopamine for pleasure and motivation, Endorphins for reducing pain and serotonin for regulating mood.

Just thinking of a person or being physically present and talking with the person releases so many hormones switching a persons in less than a minute, what should we call it attraction? Relief? Someone who brings peace?

Think in a different way why only that person? Why not others?
Why that one person makes you comfortable, relax, and makes you feel like you're everything and nothing at the same time? Yeah this is all hormone which is making you relax, reduces your stress, provides motivation, and excitement in life, pushing you in life supporting at lows like pillar, converts sad mood into happy and energetic, alertness, full high energy in work and many more. If a person is receiving this because of just being with a person then why leave?

When loving someone for just their inner person everything comes from inside there is no effort required everything is effortless like a magic, a person who is giving time and who is removing time from work just to spend that little time with the love what will you call it? Of course love.
Someone who plans everything for other without being asked, sees the person everywhere and imagines them if he/she could be here with me enjoying every moment spent in nature or some beautiful place, the art of imagining is at peak.
Sending good morning text without forget, praising the beauty, listening calmly about how the day went, isn't it all something let's call natures beauty to love. You are not expecting in return from the person instead you are only giving and the other person is also interested in you, being when you need, always keeping you at top, is that all you want and when you final get it your mind is experience what we call as love.

Isn't it beautiful what I said is all people fell and want when they are in love with someone. But what if I say you can also feel this when you love your inner person instead of loving

other person. When you fell in love for character instead of beauty it's obvious you fall for that person's inner person so the connection is internal not external. But what if your outer person starts loving your inner person?
When you are in path of self-creation creating your identity or in a process of achieving your goals it may be anything let's take an example of creating a good physique for a long run being fit in life.
So what all you need from your side? Consistency and that's it because consistency is the only key which will push you ahead every day. It's not disciple because when you are disciplined you are already consistent in your work every day here it is expected that you start working out from today.
So to start working on your goal you have to first convince your-self you have to show yourself a vision like talk to yourself look buddy our goal is to create a good physique for our benefit nothing else. We don't have to impress anyone we are doing this just for us.
Here you are talking to yourself means your inner self now you have a third person inside the love person is switched with a person who is high in energy same like you feel in gym motivating you always to lift weight, pushing you ahead always, while playing sports even sometimes you don't know you can play so well that's your inner person taking charge over you.
Love yourself when you will understand the concept what I want to say you will be unstoppable.
Do for your-self because at the end of the day it's you facing yourself with reality in your hand.
Loving yourself isn't bad but accepting your inner side and being together while working on goal is next level of happiness

you don't have worry if any one leaves you in between because you have you and if you are impressing you all those hormones will release for you.
There are so many benefits you will see while loving you.

Have you ever been in love, when we human are truly attached with a person the only thing we can feel is a change in our behavior because we want, or we hope the other person should not feel like this person is not changing as per time, this person is only focused on me and if such behavior is observed it is obvious other person will leave. But when one is truly in love there is a behavior change from inside, and you can feel it. In every aspect inner person acts like a guidance or a support system is other partner needs something we are in search and transforms ourselves as if we are provider just because that small happiness on the partners face makes us happy, someone else's happiness decides how our day will flow isn't it more like a magic?

Love, when seen beyond romance, is the most transformative force shaping both our outer and inner person. It is not only about the bond with another human being but also about the way it rewires your behavior, your energy, and your identity. When you are in love, you notice how your actions shift you become more attentive, more patient, more giving. This shift is not superficial, it is biochemical and psychological, but more importantly, it is spiritual. Love awakens a different version of you, one that is capable of extraordinary resilience and joy.

The beauty of love lies in its ability to make you step outside of yourself. Suddenly, someone else's happiness becomes your priority, and their smile dictates the rhythm of your day. You transform into a provider, a protector, a dreamer, simply because the presence of that person makes you want to be better. This is not weakness it is the magic of connection. Love teaches you that fulfillment is not found in isolation but in shared energy, in the exchange of care and trust.

Yet the deepest lesson of love is that the same transformation can happen when you direct it inward. Loving yourself is not selfish, it is foundational. When your outer person begins to love your inner person, you create a bond that is unbreakable. You stop waiting for someone else to validate your worth and begin to generate that energy from within. The hormones and emotions that flow when you are with someone you love can also flow when you nurture yourself when you invest in your health, your growth, your creativity. Self-love becomes the pillar that supports you when others leave, the flame that keeps burning even in solitude.

Love also teaches consistency. In relationships, you show up every day, you give time, you listen, and you care. The same principle applies when you love yourself. Consistency in self-love means showing up for your goals, honoring your commitments, and treating yourself with respect. It means talking to your inner person as if it were your closest companion, motivating yourself, pushing yourself, and celebrating yourself. This is how love becomes unstoppable because it is no longer dependent on someone else's presence.

The magic of love is its ability to change behavior from the inside out. When you are truly in love, whether with another person or with yourself, you feel a shift in your character. You become more generous, more resilient, and more alive. You notice how small acts sending a message, sharing a laugh, completing a workout, writing a page carry immense meaning because they are fueled by love. Love transforms ordinary routines into extraordinary experiences.

At its core, love is guidance. It is the inner person acting as a compass, showing you where to give, where to protect, where to grow. It is the force that makes you adapt, that makes you transform, and that makes you rise beyond your limitations. And when you embrace it fully both in relationships and in self-love you discover that love is not just an emotion, it is a way of living. It is the art of becoming more than you were yesterday, the joy of creating happiness for yourself and others, and the strength to keep moving forward even when life tests you.

Love, then, is not only about romance it is about identity. It is about the outer person learning to honor the inner person, about the inner person guiding the outer toward authenticity. It is about connection, whether with another soul or with your own. And once you understand this, love becomes the most powerful energy you can carry the energy that makes you unstoppable, resilient, and alive.

REGRET

Regret is one of the most powerful emotions that can consume a person after losing someone they love. Here consume is most important word. It is not just about missing their presence it is about replaying every decision, every silence, and every word spoken or left unsaid. Regret is like a shadow that follows you everywhere, whispering "what if" into your mind. What if I had stayed? What if I had listened more? What if I had given more time? These questions never stop, and they trap you in an endless loop of memories. It feels like quicksand the more you struggle, the deeper you sink.

People often spend days, weeks, even years living inside this loop, unable to move forward. They relive the happy moments, the laughter, the comfort, and then suddenly the pain strikes again because those moments are gone. Regret creates a void, and that void feels impossible to fill. It drains energy, it steals focus, and it makes you believe that happiness was only possible with that one person.

If these are all problems how can one find himself/herself if they are in stage of hurt?
How can they find their inner person their Someone Within You in these situation?

Answer is simple just by loving yourself. When you learn to love yourself, regret loses its power. You don't wake up thinking, "I should have done more for them," because the person you are investing in is you. Every effort you make is for your own growth, your own peace. Regret transforms into reflection it becomes less about pain and more about learning. Instead of drowning in memories of someone else, you build new memories with yourself: the workout you completed, the book you finished, the skill you mastered. These are not regrets, they are milestones.

Regret teaches you the importance of time and presence. It shows you how fragile moments are and how easily they slip away. But if you redirect that lesson inward, regret becomes fuel. You stop asking "why did they leave?" and start asking "what can I do today so I don't regret tomorrow?" That shift is liberation. Loving yourself means regret doesn't paralyze you it motivates you to keep moving forward, stronger than before.

Regret does not end with the memory of someone it often extends into the way you see yourself. It can make you question your worth, your choices, and even your ability to move forward. That is why regret is dangerous it convinces you that the best part of your life is already behind you. But the truth is, regret is only a reflection of what you valued most. It shows you the depth of your love, the importance of your time, and the weight of your decisions. If you can take that reflection and turn it inward, regret becomes a teacher instead of a prison.

Think about it every regret is proof that you cared. You cared enough to wish things had been different. You cared enough to replay the moments. That caring is not weakness, it is strength. It means you are capable of deep connection. But now, instead of pouring that caring into someone who is gone, you can pour it into yourself. You can care about your health, your growth, your peace. You can care about the person you are becoming. In that way, regret transforms into responsibility. It stops being about what you lost and starts being about what you can build. When you begin to love yourself, regret no longer chains you to the past. It becomes a reminder to live fully in the present. It whispers not "what if" but "what now." It tells you that every day is a chance to create moments you will not regret tomorrow. And that is the true liberation knowing that regret is not the end of your story, but the beginning of your strength.

Regret, when seen beyond its immediate sting, is a mirror that reflects both the depth of your love and the weight of your choices. It is not simply about wishing things had been different, it is about recognizing how much you cared, how much you invested, and how deeply you connected. That is why regret feels so heavy it is proof of attachment, proof of vulnerability, and proof of humanity. But regret, if left unchecked, becomes a prison. It traps you in endless loops of "what if," draining energy and convincing you that the best part of your life is already behind you.

The way forward is to transform regret into **responsibility**. Instead of replaying the past, you begin to ask: *What can I do today so I don't regret tomorrow?* This shift is powerful because it turns regret into fuel. It teaches you to value time, to honor presence, to act with intention. Every moment becomes an opportunity to create memories that will not haunt you later. Regret stops being about loss and starts being about growth.

Regret also sharpens awareness. It shows you the fragility of relationships, the importance of words, and the necessity of action. It reminds you that silence can wound as much as speech that absence can hurt as much as betrayal. These lessons, though painful, are invaluable. They teach you to be more present, more attentive, and more authentic. They teach you to live with clarity, so that tomorrow's reflection is not filled with "what if" but with "I did."

Another dimension of regret is its connection to identity. When regret strikes, it does not only question your past it questions your self-worth. It whispers that you failed, that you were not enough, that you cannot move forward. This is where self-love becomes essential. Self-lovc reframes regret not as proof of weakness but as proof of caring. It tells you: *You cared enough to wish things had been different. That caring is strength. Now direct it inward.* When you begin to care for yourself your health, your growth, your peace regret transforms into resilience.

Regret also teaches **boundaries**. It shows you where you gave too much, where you ignored your own needs, where you allowed others to define your worth. By reflecting on these patterns, you learn to protect your energy, to guard your inner child, to choose relationships that uplift rather than drain. Regret becomes a filter, clearing your path of distractions and leaving only what is essential.

The most liberating realization is that regret is temporary, but the lessons it gives are permanent. The pain fades, but the wisdom remains. Every scar becomes a reminder of resilience, every wound a story of survival. Regret, when embraced, becomes a teacher that guides you toward a fuller life. It whispers not "what if" but "what now." It tells you that every day is a chance to create moments you will not regret tomorrow.

So regret is not the end it is the beginning of strength. It is the shadow that teaches you to value light, the pain that teaches you to value presence, the loss that teaches you to value love. When you learn to listen, when you learn to redirect, regret becomes the foundation of wisdom. It becomes the voice that says: *Live fully, love deeply, and act intentionally.* And once you understand this, regret no longer chains you to the past it propels you into the future, stronger, wiser, and more alive than before.

Now let's move into **Hurt**, because regret and hurt are twins they often arrive together, but they affect you differently.

HURT

Hurt is sharper than regret. It is immediate, like a cut that bleeds before you even realize you've been wounded. When someone you love betrays you, ignores you, or simply walks away, the pain feels physical. Your chest tightens, your stomach churns, and your body reacts as if it is under attack. And in a way, it is because love rewires your brain, and losing it feels like withdrawal from a drug.

Hurt also comes from people around you who envy your growth. They act like snakes, waiting for the right moment to strike. Their words, their actions, their silence it all becomes poison. They try to pull you back, distract you, exhaust you, and cloud your vision. Their attacks may not always be direct, but they are powerful enough to shake your confidence. If you let them, they will drain your energy and stop your progress.
But when you love yourself, hurt doesn't disappear, yet it loses its control over you. You start to see clearly who belongs in your life and who doesn't. You develop observation skills reading people's intentions, recognizing patterns, and eliminating those who drain you. Hurt becomes a teacher, not

a master. It tells you: "Protect your inner child, guard your energy, and don't let anyone's negativity define your worth."

Self-love creates resilience. You stop waiting for others to heal your wounds and instead build your own armor. Hurt becomes less about destruction and more about construction it shapes you, strengthens you, and reminds you that at the end of the day, it's You vs You. And in that battle, you always have the power to win.

Hurt doesn't just test your emotions it tests your identity. It forces you to ask: *Who am I when everything I trusted is shaken?* That is the deeper layer of pain. It is not only about what someone did to you, but about how you see yourself after it. Hurt can make you doubt your strength, your worth, and even your ability to continue. But this is where self-love becomes the turning point. When you begin to love yourself, hurt transforms from a wound into a signal. It tells you where you must grow, where you must protect, and where you must let go. Instead of collapsing under the weight of betrayal or rejection, you rise with awareness. You start to understand that hurt is not proof of weakness it is proof of how deeply you cared. And caring is never wrong. What matters is where you direct that care next.

Hurt also teaches boundaries. It shows you who deserves your energy and who does not. It sharpens your vision so you can recognize patterns those who uplift you versus those who drain you. It teaches you to walk away from people who only bring poison, and to walk closer to those who bring peace. In this way, hurt becomes a filter. It clears your path of distractions and leaves only what is essential.

The most powerful realization is that hurt is temporary, but the lessons it gives are permanent. Every scar becomes a reminder of resilience. Every wound becomes a story of survival. And every time you choose to heal yourself instead of waiting for someone else to heal you, you build armor that no one can break. At the end of the day, hurt is part of the journey. It is not the end it is the beginning of strength. When you embrace it, when you learn from it, when you rise above it, you discover that the battle was never against others. It was always You vs You. And once you understand that, you stop fearing hurt, because you know you already have the power to win.

Hurt, when expanded beyond the immediate sting, becomes a profound teacher of resilience, identity, and boundaries. It is sharper than regret because it arrives suddenly, without warning, and forces you to confront truths you may have ignored. But the missing dimension in understanding hurt is how it evolves over time how the wound that feels unbearable in the moment becomes a scar that carries wisdom, how the pain that shakes your identity becomes the foundation of your strength.

The missing topic is also the **role of forgiveness**. Hurt often lingers because we hold on to anger, replaying the betrayal or rejection. Forgiveness does not mean excusing the harm, it means releasing yourself from its grip. It is an act of self-love, a way of reclaiming energy that would otherwise be drained by resentment. The inner person guides this process, whispering that forgiveness is not for them it is for you. It is the key to transforming hurt from poison into medicine.

Boundaries are another lesson hurt teaches with clarity. When someone crosses your limits, when their words or actions wound you, hurt becomes the signal that boundaries must be set. It sharpens your vision, helping you distinguish between those who uplift and those who drain. Boundaries are not walls, they are filters. They allow love in while keeping toxicity out. Hurt is the experience that teaches you where those filters must be placed.

Hurt also connects to resilience through repetition. The first wound feels unbearable, but over time, as you face hurt again and again, you learn that survival is possible. Each scar becomes a reminder of strength, each healed wound a story of endurance. Hurt becomes less about destruction and more about construction it shapes you, strengthens you, and reminds you that at the end of the day, it is always *You vs You*. The inner person thrives in this battle, teaching you that resilience is not about avoiding pain but about rising after it.

Finally, hurt reveals the impermanence of pain and permanence of lessons. The sting fades, the wound heals, but the wisdom remains. Every scar carries a message: protect your energy, guard your inner child, trust yourself more than others, and never let negativity define your worth. Hurt is temporary, but the awareness it brings is eternal. It teaches you to walk away from poison, to walk closer to peace, to choose self-love over self-doubt.

So when you think of hurt, do not see it only as suffering. See it as a signal, a teacher, a filter, a paradox, a builder of resilience. It is sharper than regret, but it is also richer in lessons. It tests your emotions, your identity, your boundaries, and your strength. And when you embrace it, when you learn from it, when you rise above it, you discover that hurt was never meant to destroy you it was meant to awaken you. The battle was never against others, it was always *You vs You*. And once you understand that, you stop fearing hurt, because you know you already have the power to win.

ENERGY

After that one person leaves you people are still busy in putting efforts yeah that's good if you are fighting but if the person wants to come back why would the person leave? It means you are lacking somewhere or you are getting distracted from your life any reason it might be analyze the situation why it happened with you. If you got the answer start working on yourself and fix the problem at the exact moment so next time you won't suffer again. Learn from your mistakes. After the person eaves you don't waste your energy if you know the person won't come back your energy preservation your mental peace is more important. Why to invest in something which gives back literally zero profit?

The best place to invest energy is you.

You got free time start exercising or read, invest that free time instead of just passing that time. I read a quote the precious thing human have in his life is time. You have it

Use it because it won't come back. Later what you will do is only regret of not utilizing it.

Today you have energy invest in you, you are feeling high do heavy workout session, you are feeling happy do what you love

to do I personally grab my laptop and start writing. Later what you get the result is worth it all those hormones which we talked about love will release for you.
You will feel happy trust me you will pat your back for investing that time and energy instead of wasting it.

Who said don't love? Everyone has right to love but your first priority should be yourself. The person sitting in you make him/her happy all you want all you crave do it instantly for yourself, you feel like eating ice cream at 12pm go do it right at that moment for yourself, you feel like spending time in nature go do some trek spend time for your-self because,
At the end of the day it's you facing yourself with reality in your hand.

No one is free in their life to understand you all the time people will free their time to feel you but they won't understand you because they also have themselves to impress.
Just think why would someone invest their time in you? Unless the person loves in that case the person gets those hormones kick by your presence in their life now that's a little different concept.
Just identify your inner side, you know how you are from inside like someone who easily gets hurt by other person and they fell deep inside then you must hide your inner side and focus on yourself love yourself. That child must not get hurt that's your someone within your, for that inner person's happiness you are doing this everything.
Remember those days when you're sleeping and you are proud of yourself by the work you did all day. For whom is that all happiness? Of course you that's what your ultimate goal.

At any place any moment your feeling, your satisfaction matter most to you.

Energy is the currency of life. Every thought, every action, every emotion spends energy. The question is: where are you investing it? Many people waste energy chasing someone who has already walked away. They spend nights thinking, days waiting, and weeks hoping. That energy gives no return it is like pouring water into sand.

But when you redirect energy into yourself, everything changes. Energy invested in growth multiplies. A single workout builds strength for tomorrow. A single page written becomes part of a book. A single hour of learning becomes knowledge that lasts a lifetime. Energy invested in yourself compounds it grows, it expands, and it creates momentum.

Think of energy as fire. If you give it to someone who doesn't value it, it burns out quickly. But if you feed it into your own goals, it becomes a flame that lights your path. That flame keeps you warm when others leave, it keeps you focused when distractions come, and it keeps you alive when challenges rise.

The truth is, energy is more important than time. Time passes whether you use it or not, but energy decides how that time feels. A single hour with high energy can achieve more than a whole day with low energy. That is why self-love is powerful it keeps your energy alive. It gives you motivation, focus, and joy even when no one else is around.

At the end of the day, regret, hurt, and energy are all connected. Regret drains energy, hurt misdirects energy, but self-love restores energy. When you love yourself, regret becomes wisdom, hurt becomes strength, and energy becomes growth. That is the cycle of transformation. That is how you become unstoppable.

Energy is not just fuel for action it is the essence of presence. Every thought, every emotion, every decision spends energy. That is why introverts guard it carefully, why overthinking drains it invisibly, and why silence restores it. Extroverts may scatter energy outward, drawing strength from crowds, while introverts concentrate energy inward, drawing strength from solitude. But regardless of personality, the principle remains: energy must be invested wisely.

The missing topic is **energy as focus**. Distraction is the greatest thief of energy. When you chase people who have already left, when you replay regrets endlessly, when you allow hurt to dominate your mind, you are scattering energy into places that give no return. It is like pouring water into sand it disappears without nourishing anything. Focus redirects energy into growth. A single workout, a single page written, a single hour of learning compounds into strength, creativity, and wisdom. Energy invested in yourself multiplies, while energy wasted on emptiness evaporates.

Energy also teaches boundaries. Every interaction is a transaction, and not all transactions are profitable. Some people drain energy with negativity, envy, or manipulation. Others uplift you, inspire you, and multiply your energy. Hurt sharpens this vision, teaching you to filter who deserves your energy and who does not. Boundaries are not selfish they are strategic. They ensure your energy is preserved for what truly matters: your growth, your peace, your inner person.

Another missing layer is energy as transformation. Regret drains energy, hurt misdirects energy, but self-love restores energy. When you love yourself, regret becomes wisdom, hurt becomes strength, and energy becomes growth. This cycle of transformation is the essence of resilience. It shows that energy is not static it can be redirected, recharged, and renewed. Even when you feel drained, silence, solitude, and creativity can restore your flame.

Think of energy as fire. If you give it to someone who doesn't value it, it burns out quickly. But if you feed it into your own goals, it becomes a flame that lights your path. That flame keeps you warm when others leave, keeps you focused when distractions come, and keeps you alive when challenges rise. Energy is more important than time because time passes whether you use it or not, but energy decides how that time feels. A single hour with high energy can achieve more than a whole day with low energy.

Energy also connects to **identity**. How you spend energy defines who you are. If you invest it in negativity, you become bitter. If you invest it in growth, you become strong. If you invest it in love, you become compassionate. The outer person is shaped by how the inner person directs energy. And the inner person is strengthened when the outer person uses energy wisely. This is the curve of life the dance between inner and outer, between preservation and expression, between solitude and connection.

At the end of the day, energy is the thread that ties together regret, hurt, resilience, and growth. It is the invisible currency that decides whether your life feels abundant or empty. The "Someone Within You" is the guardian of this energy, whispering when to give and when to withdraw, when to shine and when to rest. It reminds you that energy is sacred, that it must be preserved, protected, and invested in yourself first. Because when you are strong, when your flame is alive, you can share it with others without losing yourself.

So do not fear hurt, do not drown in regret, and do not scatter energy into emptiness. Redirect it inward. Invest it in your growth, your creativity, your peace. Let energy become your fire, your currency, your compass. And remember: at the end of the day, it is always *You vs You*. The battle is not about whether you have energy it is about where you choose to spend it. And once you learn to invest it in yourself, you become unstoppable.

Acceptance

After understanding the concept of loving yourself, the next step is acceptance. Accepting yourself from within. You may love your inner side, but it is equally important to understand what you are trying to give yourself, does your inner self truly want it? **Both your acceptance and your inner person's acceptance matter.**

Understanding yourself is the biggest challenge. For example, in life someone may have body-shamed you, teased your communication skills, or mocked you in front of a group. This happens to many people while growing up. Some take it lightly and let it go, but others feel hurt inside, as if a void is created, and they never forget the insult. At such moments, they are not in the mental state for understanding and acceptance. If the person is naturally understanding, it would not create such turmoil in the mind. Whatever was said may have been reality a direct slap on self-belief. The body shaming wasn't just a joke, it was reality. The communication taunt wasn't just a joke, it was reality too. A real person would accept everything: "Whatever was said is truth, I need to work on myself, stay physically fit, and improve my impression in public." People judge first by appearance and communication, even from a distance. Understanding this is basic, so ideally no one should be hurt by such taunts, though it is difficult to accept.

As this was an example, dear readers, you must accept in the same way about your inner person. Others may say you are strong inside, confident in your decisions. But they don't know your reality. They see strength, but only you know your weakness. Even the strongest person feels weak at times, lacking emotional support, wishing for someone to listen and stand beside them. Yet you don't get carried away but you fight alone, smile outside, but cry inside. Isn't that acceptance? Inside you there isn't just one person. There are thousands of personalities, and you must accept them all. When you felt low but didn't show it to friends or family, it was because someone inside you gave you strength.

Tap your back for a moment, appreciate your inner side for being with you when no one else was. These times shape you. They are obstacles placed by nature for your benefit. Don't question them instead face them. Every day won't meet your expectations. Some days will be low, some joyful, some mixed. At every moment ask yourself: what do my body and mind want? At times their demands will differ, creating confusion. Who will accept then?

In boxing matches, fighters often tire, and their ability to make decisions and create tactics fades as the mind shuts down, yet the body keeps fighting. Similarly, while driving long distances, many have experienced this: on a smooth road with little traffic, the mind drifts into sleep mode, like a laptop active but not fully. Then a sudden speed breaker wakes the mind in shock. The first thought is: how far did I drive while my mind was asleep? After that, the mind gives 200% to stay awake for survival. The reality is, during those moments in boxing or driving, it was the physical body that didn't give up. We call it muscle memory. Even when you have no power left, someone inside you never gives up and always holds you when you fall and you must accept that.

Accept and move on:

In everyone's life you must have gone through a moment where you meet a person started talking and somehow you became very close to each other and later a time comes where one has to go and other is not in a state to accept what is happening why the person is leaving?

It has become a habit of attraction where day feels heavy without communication with that one person but its law of nature everyone is not meant to be permanent still they try to be permanent till they have access to be together. Accept when they are gone means they are gone forever, it is said if two people aren't written to meet again they won't meet at any cost until nature allows them to.

But if you want to meet yourself who is stopping you?

Even nature can't stop you meeting yourself accept the fact. Instead of being emotional dependent on others be dependent on yourself you know very well this person won't kill mine trust and will be with me forever then use it for your benefits. We are going to discuss further about this topic for now just think of you are blind having stick in your hand and you are walking on street so for blind people a special track is made of guiding block which have raised patters that can be felt through

their stick and also foot helping to walk but at some place if such track are not built, How will you walk?
Some professional blind people, I mean to say those people who are trained such people have good hearing ability which makes them very sensitive and they analyze the surrounding in better way which makes them easy to walk where guiding block are absent.

At such point in life when no one is around you for your support guiding block is also absent whom will you trust? The only close person you have is you yourself. Imagine the amount of power they require to step out of house when you can't see only trusting the stick in hand and ears, because they have accepted themselves and the amount of trust they have on themselves makes them take step outside house.
I have a friend who is physically handicapped and his both legs don't work he can't apply his body weight on his legs so he uses sticks all day still he travels everyday alone climbs stairs, walks and he does this every day.
What makes him do this every day?

He's self-belief, accepting everything and without giving excuses he steps out and lives he's life at all best.
Acceptance an understanding is so powerful even you fail still you won't regret. All problems vanish like they didn't exist in your life whatever is happening in your life now it may be good or bad, sad or happy anything which happened in past which you are still carrying in your present just accept it. Just doing this one thing will eliminate your maximum questions roaming in mind. You know yourself so accept that's you, ever

something bad happened with you accept as karma and move on.

The day you accept yourself, your inner self will be your best friend supporting you in every phase of life.

Understanding

We have talked about acceptance, but understanding is just as important. Understanding is a form of acceptance, and accepting is a form of understanding. In daily life you will face challenges, small to big, but some problems will suddenly appear and leave you in shock. "Why is it always me who faces consequences?" Such questions are common in this phase. But instead of questioning, accept the situation and try to understand it. Look back and connect the dots and you will see patterns forming, and realize everything you went through was for your benefit, planned by nature. This shows how good you are at accepting and understanding yourself and your surroundings.

Understanding yourself doesn't mean knowing everything, it means accepting your pros and cons. Your inner side has both good and bad, and you know it well. Think of how your thoughts change in anger, wishing bad for someone even though you are a green flag inside and outside. Situations can transform you temporarily, but it's not necessary to take it seriously or get carried away. One day I was playing cricket in college with four friends. We played daily, but once we faced juniors who played better and we were losing. I went to bat after a wicket since the order wasn't fixed, but one friend argued he would bat instead. In cricket you must fight till the last ball, even when losing, but he didn't agree. We argued in front of everyone, shouting from strike to non-strike while batting. After that, we didn't talk. Later I realized incidents occur as per the situation, and instead of overthinking, you just have to accept and understand its past, focus on the present.

This is maturity: to understand yourself, your surroundings, and react accordingly. It leaves a print of your personality, showing others what kind of person you are your outer self.

Take a look around, inside, and at the people you spend most of your time with. Ask yourself questions you will find answers. Readers, this book *Someone Within You* is non-fiction, self-help, self-development. It doesn't mean reading it will instantly motivate you or make you great. Many expect a comeback after reading self-help, but the truth is: people start reading when they are unsure about their inner self, their potential, and their self-belief. When you feel lonely, I ask why? You have yourself, your inner self. Work, exercise, and grow together with your inner person. Do it for the one inside you. When you realize that power, you will stop relying on self-help books. Whenever you have an idea, try to implement it even a prototype shows the world your thought made reality.

Recently I had an idea for a 2D board game. First, I researched if it already existed. After weeks of planning rules, board design, number of players, I told a friend, and we decided to build it. Did I gather motivation? No. Did I ask negative questions like "Can I do it? I'm new in game development"? No. I simply talked with myself. Our next chapter is *Talk with Yourself*. For now, it means communicating with your inner self as you would with a friend sharing problems, casual talks, and jokes. Your inner self is a person without physical appearance. I asked myself positive questions: "How can I do it? Which engine should I use? When should I start?" Such questions push you forward, increasing self-belief. Next time you have an idea, your first thought will be: "How can I make it possible? How can I prototype it?" That is understanding. This book won't show you the path it gives you tools. You must decide how to use them.

Any self-help book is the same. It shows reality from the surface, like seeing water in a well from above. Only when you jump in do you realize its depth. True understanding comes when you apply lessons in life. Books guide, but transformation happens when you practice, reflect, and adapt advice to your context.

Every event in life has a reason, pre-written by nature. If something isn't meant for you, even giving 200% won't change it you will lose and question. But when you implement acceptance and understanding, most problems vanish. Overthinking, anxiety, and stress reduce. Look around years pass, everything changes: environment, people, and personality. Life is like a plant: a flower blooms, lives its day, dies, and the next day a new flower blooms. Every day is your new year, your new birth. The plant doesn't know if it will get sunlight or water, yet it grows to full potential. Humans should be the same.

Nature gives opportunities it's you who must notice. One night I was questioning myself: "What am I doing? What new can I do?" My eyes fell on my laptop, then my books poems, non-fiction, self-help. A voice inside said: "Pushkar, you are good at writing, you have resources, why not start a book?" With knowledge from authors and personal experience, I knew it would help readers. In the same way, you also have resources look around, start your work, believe in nature and yourself. Do it for the person inside you. Acceptance is everything, understanding is truth.

When you accept your inner person and understand its reason, presence, and way of being, you grasp the concept of *Someone Within You*. Daily life brings questions some push, some pull. One decision can change your life.

Keep this line forever: *A single decision can change a person's life.*

The only one who stands with you in your lowest and your happiness is yourself the child inside you. At the end of the day, your mental peace matters most.

Surrender

Whenever we hear the word *surrender*, the first thought that comes to mind is giving up, losing, or facing defeat. At the beginning of *Outer Person* I said to understand *Someone Within You*, you must change your vision. In the same way, change how you look at surrender.

It was the last week of December, and the reason I was writing this book I lost it. Just like Spider-Man's sense warns him when something is wrong, I had a strong feeling something was wrong. I knew I was going to lose something. But instead of focusing on the problem, I continued writing. In the last week, I finally lost it completely. What should I do now? Should I continue writing my book? Such questions began to arise in my mind.

It was December, a holiday month. My friends were planning trips, treks, internships, earning money. On the other hand, here I was writing a book a completely different hobby. I felt lost by the action nature took on me. I was hoping for the expected reward, but as I said earlier, everything happens according to nature's plan. You cannot deny or change the process. The only option is to accept and go through it.

The feeling I had that something was going to change was the phase of traveling from point A to point B, as I showed in the diagram. Later I realized why I felt that way: my goal was the expected reward, but nature wanted me to have the real reward, so it ensured I traveled the correct path. It's like boarding the right train at the station, but when you look outside the window, the train moves in the opposite direction of your destination. Even though it's the correct train, the direction feels wrong. My goal was shifting, and I ignored the feeling. But what can you do in such a moment? In the end, nature always has something beautiful for you.

With this thought, I sat quietly one day, closed my eyes, recalled past events, and started connecting the dots arranging them in order to create a pattern. Why am I here, in this situation? I searched for the answer, and I was right I found it. It took me a week, but I was happy in the end. During that phase of finding new purpose, the only thing I did was surrender giving myself totally, handing everything to nature. That day I said one line to nature: *"From now, whichever path you show me, I am ready to walk on it."*

I have observed how people bring their ego when they must surrender, and that is not the behavior expected. You will understand the whole concept after reading *Inner Person* the whole book. A person should be like a river: always in flow, calm, relaxed. These should be the upper qualities of a person.

Whenever someone meets you, they should feel your outer person is calm and good in behavior, like a green forest. For such a person, surrender is nothing it's like asking them to donate a single hair strand, which is no loss at all.

I understand surrender is not easy. While writing this topic, I remembered past moments when I gave up and surrendered myself, praying to nature to take away everything I once prayed for. Then a question came: what is the difference between surrender and giving up? I wasn't looking for a dictionary definition I could Google that. But Googling everything is not efficient. So I decided to ask nature and figure out the answer in my surroundings.

Surrender is often misunderstood because we equate it with defeat, but in truth surrender is not about losing it is about releasing. When you surrender, you are not throwing away your strength, you are shifting it. You are saying: *I trust the flow more than I trust my resistance.* That is why surrender feels so difficult because ego wants control, ego wants certainty, and ego wants to dictate the outcome. But nature, life, the universe whatever name you give it always has a larger plan than your ego can imagine.

The difference between surrender and giving up lies in intention. Giving up is born from exhaustion, from hopelessness, from the belief that nothing can change. It is passive, heavy, and rooted in despair. Surrender, on the other hand, is active. It is a conscious choice to let go of control and allow life to guide you. When you surrender, you are not saying "I quit." You are saying "I trust." That trust is not weakness it is wisdom. Think of water flowing in a river. If you fight against the current, you exhaust yourself, you lose energy, and you may even drown. But if you surrender to the current, you move forward effortlessly. You may not know exactly where the river will take you, but you know it will carry you. That is surrender. It is not defeat it is alignment.

In my own reflection, I realized surrender is a doorway. It opens you to paths you never planned, experiences you never expected, and lessons you never imagined. When I surrendered, I discovered that the reward I was chasing was not the real reward. The real reward was growth, clarity, and the ability to see beyond my own expectations. That is why surrender is powerful it transforms loss into discovery.

Surrender is not the end of effort it is the beginning of flow. It teaches your patience, humility, and trust. It reminds you that you are not alone in your journey, that there is a larger intelligence guiding you. And when you surrender, you stop fighting battles that were never yours to fight. You conserve energy, you protect peace, and you allow yourself to grow in ways control could never achieve. So the next time surrender arrives in your life, don't see it as defeat. See it as transformation. See it as the moment when you stop clinging to the illusion of control and start embracing the truth of flow. Because surrender is not about losing it is about finding. It is about finding yourself, your path, and your strength in the very act of letting go.

TALK WITH YOURSELF

In your life there must have been a moment when you talked with yourself, asked questions, or had casual conversations like you do with friends, and the relief you felt afterward was completely worth it. In my childhood I did the same whenever I felt alone with no one around. Sometimes talking with yourself makes loneliness vanish, and though some may think its foolish, trust me, it's not.

Talking with yourself means communicating with your inner self, and you must do this daily to understand yourself and perform tasks professionally without anyone's help. When I am assigned a task and get stuck, the first step I take is analyzing why I cannot move forward. Then I ask myself, "Hey buddy, this is where I'm stuck, could you help?" My inner self responds with questions: "Have you tried this? Have you done that?" The benefit of asking yourself questions is that it makes complex work easier to understand.

It's not only about work but also about low moments. As I write this, it is the first week of January 2026, so happy New Year to all my readers. When the year began, I was confused, my brain overthinking: will all this effort pay off? I am a college student, and December was my vacation month. I spent it writing this book, determined to publish my first work. But as 2026 started, doubts filled my mind. The purpose I was writing for was gone. It was hard to accept.

I asked myself: instead of writing, should I have invested time in building myself physically, learning a technical course, or a new programming language? Regret weighed on me. Yet instead of drowning in it, I gave myself one or two days to calm down. In those days I learned that humans complicate simple things by overthinking. I followed Premanand Maharaj's advice, and my regret vanished. If I have invested time in one task, why leave it halfway? I realized nature always has answers. There was a reason I lost my purpose it was teaching me. This understanding came only when I calmly asked myself questions.

Everything in life is written by nature. You cannot deny its decisions. When an event must occur, it will, and you will question why, what, and how. But trust nature's plan, it always has something beautiful for you, even if it takes away your peace. From my experience, I can say you'll gain something more stable.

At first, you won't see the patterns. Your mind will confuse you, stress will rise, and questions will circle. This phase is not easy it is your battle with yourself. At such moments, do nothing. Calm yourself, give time, and slowly the dots will connect. You will see the patterns nature has made for you.

Question yourself to calm your mind.
I asked my inner self:
Me: Buddy, what is this test nature is taking me through? What is it teaching me?
Inner self: Don't worry Pushkar, I am with you. Don't overthink, just stay calm.
Me: Did I make a mistake by investing my whole month in this book?
Inner self: No Pushkar, you did what you planned for months. Now you're halfway and thinking to leave?
Me: But I lost my purpose, what about that?

Inner self: Losing purpose is not a big deal. Just change your purpose. Write this book for yourself.

After this conversation, I found answers to most of my questions. When I started writing for myself, the dots connected. I saw why I lost my purpose it was a distraction. Nature ensured I completed my book without distraction. I was busy questioning why, but now I have no regret, no doubt just me, my inner self, and nature moving forward together.

This is what I want to tell you: communicate with yourself, talk with your inner self, and most importantly, don't tell anyone you do it. I once read a line: "You were busy searching for the lock's key in your whole house, and the key was in your hand." In the same way, you already have solutions, but your mind is not calm enough to see them. That's why the saying goes: think with a calm mind.

From day to night you run, searching for peace, but it is already inside you, inside your home. If you believe in God, leave everything in his hands your life is already written. On this path, you have only two companions: God and your inner self. Whenever you visit a temple to pray, what are you praying for? Either blessings or requests. But when you can do the same with your inner self, why visit a temple? It is all for mental acceptance.

We have already discussed acceptance and understanding. When you visit a temple during tough times and pray for peace, your mind accepts and understands that everything will be fine. In reality, it depends on you. The temple provides mental calmness, and in that state, the brain searches for solutions. But imagine if you made yourself a temple. Wouldn't it be magical? At any place you could take blessings, solve problems, and find peace. That is possible. I personally carry a temple within me, so in chaos I remain calm because of daily communication with my inner self. Take it as a blessing whatever you have today, you deserve. Don't lose it or ignore it. Thank nature for your resources, because many struggle daily to achieve them.

Even after reading this book, if you feel like you met yourself, congratulations you have found a companion who will be with you forever. You are not alone.

I watch daily blogs of mh45rider, a man from a rural area who decided to cycle across North India. He traveled 30,000 km across three countries. Imagine: cycling daily, editing videos alone, shooting alone, exploring places, and sharing them with the world. He always talks with himself because he trusts his inner person. I met him personally at Anjaneri Fort in Nashik, the birthplace of Lord Hanuman. Watching him set up his camera, shoot, and move forward impressed me deeply. Behind the camera we don't see his struggles, but he surely faces many. He meets fans daily, talks with them, and engages on social media. He is not alone in his journey but none of this is possible without self-belief and trust in oneself.

Why Talking to Yourself Matters

Talking to yourself is often misunderstood. Society sometimes labels it as odd, eccentric, or even a sign of weakness, but in truth, it is the most profound act of self-awareness. The dialogue you hold within shapes your emotions, decisions, and destiny far more than any external conversation ever could. When you speak to yourself, you are not performing for an audience, nor are you trying to impress or persuade anyone. You are engaging in the rawest form of honesty, a dialogue stripped of masks and pretenses. Meditation becomes the sacred space where this dialogue transforms from scattered thoughts into meaningful communication. It is here that you discover the true importance of talking to yourself not as a habit of isolation, but as a practice of connection.

The reason self-talk matters so deeply is that it reveals the architecture of your inner world. Every belief you hold, every fear you nurture, every dream you chase is constructed through the words you whisper to yourself. If those words are negative, they build walls of doubt and insecurity. If they are positive, they construct bridges of courage and resilience. Meditation allows you to step back and observe this construction process. It slows down the pace of your thoughts so you can see the foundations being laid. You begin to notice how often you criticize yourself, how often you encourage yourself, and how often you silence yourself. This awareness is the first step toward transformation, because you cannot change what you do not see.

Talking to yourself also matters because it is the only dialogue that cannot be deceived. In conversations with others, you may hide your true feelings, exaggerate your strengths, or downplay your weaknesses. But when you speak to yourself, especially in meditation, there is no hiding. You may try to deny certain truths, but silence has a way of revealing them. You may try to avoid certain emotions, but awareness has a way of confronting them. This honesty is uncomfortable at times, but it is liberating. It frees you from illusions and grounds you in reality. It teaches you that growth begins not with external validation but with internal recognition.

Meditation deepens this dialogue by creating a rhythm of listening and responding. In silence, you ask yourself questions: *What do I truly want? Why am I restless? What am I afraid of?* These questions are not rhetorical, they are invitations. And the answers come, not always in words, but in feelings, images, or sudden clarity. You may feel a sense of peace when you acknowledge your truth, or a surge of energy when you recognize your strength. These responses are the language of the inner self, and meditation teaches you to interpret them. Over time, you realize that talking to yourself is not a monologue but a dialogue a conversation between your conscious mind and your deeper self.

The importance of this dialogue extends beyond personal growth, it influences every aspect of your life. When you talk to yourself with kindness, you cultivate resilience. When you talk to yourself with clarity, you make better decisions. When you talk to yourself with courage, you face challenges with strength. This inner dialogue becomes the foundation of your outer actions. It shapes the way you interact with others, the way you pursue your goals, and the way you respond to setbacks. In this sense, talking to yourself is not selfish, it is essential. It ensures that your outer life is aligned with your inner truth.

Meditation transforms self-talk into a ritual of empowerment. Instead of letting your thoughts wander aimlessly, you guide them with awareness. You replace criticism with compassion, doubt with encouragement, and confusion with clarity. Each session becomes a rehearsal for life, a practice of speaking to yourself in ways that uplift rather than diminish. Over time, this practice rewires your mind. You begin to notice that your default dialogue shifts from negativity to positivity, from fear to courage, from chaos to calm. This shift is not superficial, it is profound. It changes the way you see yourself, and in turn, the way you see the world.

Ultimately, talking to yourself matters because it is the only dialogue that lasts a lifetime. Friends may come and go, mentors may guide you for a season, but the inner voice remains. It is with you in moments of triumph and in moments of despair. It is with you when you wake in the morning and when you fall asleep at night. Meditation ensures that this lifelong companion is not neglected but nurtured. It teaches you to listen, to respond, and to trust. It reminds you that the most important conversation you will ever have is not with the world but with yourself. And when that conversation is honest, compassionate, and empowering, it becomes the foundation of a life lived with authenticity and purpose.

Remember readers, in chapter, "Meditation" I have told you we will cover rest part of meditation in 3rd chapter, "Talk with Yourself". Now its time to continue it, let's talk about ways by which one can find his inner person by using meditation.

Meditation as Messenger

Meditation is often described as silence, but in truth it is a messenger. It carries signals from the deeper layers of your being to the surface of your awareness. In daily life, your conscious mind is busy planning, worrying, reacting, and constantly processing the external world. Beneath this surface lies the subconscious, a reservoir of intuition, memory, and wisdom that often remains unheard. Meditation delivers messages between these two realms. It is the bridge that allows your conscious awareness to receive guidance from the deeper self. When you sit in silence, breathing with awareness, you are essentially opening the mailbox of your soul, waiting for letters written in the language of intuition. These letters may not arrive in words, they may come as feelings, images, or sudden clarity. Yet they are messages nonetheless, carrying truths that shape your life.

The breath becomes the language of this messenger. Each inhale is like a question posed to the inner self, and each exhale is like an answer returned. Silence becomes the medium through which these messages travel. Unlike spoken language, silence does not distort meaning, it preserves it. Awareness becomes the connection that ensures the message is received. Without awareness, the letters remain unopened, the guidance unread. Meditation teaches you to cultivate awareness so that you can recognize and interpret the messages being sent. Over time, you realize that meditation is not passive, it is active communication. It is the daily act of checking in with your inner self, of reading the letters that guide your growth and destiny.

This messenger role of meditation is transformative because it changes the way you relate to yourself. Instead of seeing your thoughts as random noise, you begin to see them as signals. Instead of dismissing your feelings as distractions, you begin to see them as messages. Even restlessness becomes a message, telling you that something within needs attention. Even joy becomes a message, affirming that you are aligned with your truth. Meditation teaches you to listen to these messages without judgment, to accept them as guidance rather than resist them as obstacles. In this way, meditation becomes a dialogue, a two-way communication between the conscious and the subconscious, between the outer self and the inner self.

Consider how often in life we ignore messages from within. We feel exhausted but push ourselves harder. We sense unease in a relationship but silence the intuition. We feel inspired by a dream but dismiss it as impractical. These ignored messages accumulate, creating disconnection and confusion. Meditation restores the connection. It teaches you to pause, to listen, and to honor the messages being sent. It reminds you that your inner self is not against you but for you, always guiding you toward growth and fulfillment.

Meditation as messenger also reveals the interconnectedness of life. The messages you receive are not isolated, they are influenced by nature, relationships, and experiences. When you meditate in nature, the messages become clearer. The rustling of leaves becomes part of the dialogue, reminding you of patience. The flowing of rivers becomes part of the dialogue, teaching you to let go. The stillness of mountains becomes part of the dialogue, showing you stability. In silence, you realize that the inner self is not isolated but deeply connected to the universe. Meditation delivers not only personal messages but universal ones, reminding you of your place in the larger whole.

The messenger role of meditation also extends to destiny. The messages you receive are not random, they are guidance toward your path. Destiny is not imposed from outside, it is shaped from within. Meditation ensures that you are not drifting aimlessly but walking consciously, guided by the Someone Within You. This guidance is subtle but powerful. It may not tell you exactly what to do, but it reveals what feels true. It may not provide a map, but it offers a compass. By following this compass, you shape a destiny that is authentic, purposeful, and fulfilling. Meditation becomes the practice that ensures your destiny is not accidental but intentional, not imposed but chosen.

Meditation as messenger also teaches patience. Messages from within do not always arrive immediately. Sometimes they take time, like letters delayed in the mail. You may sit in silence and feel nothing, hear nothing, sense nothing. But this does not mean the messenger is absent. It means the message is being prepared. Over time, with persistence, the messages arrive. They may come suddenly, in a flash of insight, or gradually, in a slow unfolding. Meditation teaches you to trust the process, to wait for the messages, to believe that they will come.

In practical terms, meditation as messenger can be experienced through simple rituals. Begin each session by asking a question: *What do I need today? What am I resisting? What is my truth?* Sit in silence, breathe with awareness, and wait for the response. Do not force it, allow it to arise naturally. The response may come as a feeling of calm, a sudden thought, or a shift in perspective. Trust it. Write it down if you wish, as a letter from your inner self. Over time, these letters form a dialogue, a record of your growth, a testament to the guidance of the messenger.

Ultimately, meditation as messenger is about relationship. It is about building intimacy with yourself, learning to trust your own voice, and honoring your own truth. This relationship is the most important one you will ever have, because it shapes all others. When you are in dialogue with yourself, you are less dependent on external validation. You no longer seek approval from others because you have found approval within. You no longer fear rejection because you have accepted yourself. You no longer feel lost because you are guided by the Someone Within You.

Meditation is not about escaping life, it is about entering it more deeply. It is not about silencing the mind, it is about hearing the soul. It is not about becoming someone else, it is about meeting the Someone Within You who has always been there, waiting to guide you. As messenger, meditation ensures that you are not disconnected but connected, not lost but guided, not silent but in dialogue. It is the daily act of receiving letters from your soul, of reading the messages that shape your destiny, of living in alignment with your truth.

Meditation and Destiny

Destiny is a word that carries both mystery and weight. For centuries, people have debated whether destiny is predetermined by forces beyond our control or shaped by the choices we make. Meditation offers a profound perspective on this question. It reveals that destiny is neither entirely fixed nor entirely random, it is a living path shaped by the dialogue between your inner self and the outer world. Meditation becomes the practice that ensures you are not drifting aimlessly but walking consciously, guided by the "Someone Within You."

When you meditate, you begin to see destiny not as a distant event but as a daily unfolding. Each breath, each moment of awareness, each insight becomes a step along the path. Meditation teaches you that destiny is not something waiting at the end of life but something created in every choice you make. The messages you receive in silence those subtle whispers of intuition, those flashes of clarity are the compass points that guide you. They do not dictate your path, but they illuminate it. They remind you of your values, your strengths, and your truth, ensuring that your destiny is authentic rather than accidental.

Meditation shapes destiny by aligning your actions with your inner self. In daily life, it is easy to be swayed by external influences society's expectations, peer pressure, or fleeting desires. These influences can lead you away from your true path, creating a destiny that feels hollow or disconnected. Meditation restores alignment. It teaches you to pause before acting, to listen inward before responding, to consult the inner guide before making decisions. This alignment ensures that your destiny reflects who you truly are, not who others expect you to be. It transforms destiny from a product of circumstance into a creation of authenticity.

Destiny is also shaped by resilience, and meditation cultivates resilience by connecting you with the inner self. Life is full of challenges loss, failure, rejection, uncertainty. These challenges can derail your path if you rely solely on external support. But meditation reminds you that you carry within you a source of strength that cannot be taken away. The Someone Within You offers comfort in despair, courage in fear, and stability in chaos. This resilience ensures that obstacles do not destroy your destiny but refine it. Each challenge becomes a lesson, each setback a stepping stone, each difficulty a message guiding you forward.

Meditation also reveals that destiny is not linear. It is not a straight path from beginning to end but a journey with twists, turns, and detours. Sometimes you feel certain of your direction, only to encounter unexpected changes. Meditation teaches you to embrace these changes, to trust that even detours have meaning. In silence, you realize that destiny is not about reaching a specific destination but about living authentically along the way. The path may change, but the compass remains the same: the inner self guiding you toward truth.

Another way meditation shapes destiny is through clarity. Confusion is one of the greatest obstacles to living authentically. When you are confused, you hesitate, procrastinate, or make choices that do not reflect your values. Meditation dissolves confusion by creating space for clarity. In silence, the noise fades, and the truth emerges. You begin to see what matters, what does not, what is real, what is illusion. This clarity ensures that your destiny is not shaped by confusion but by truth. It allows you to act with confidence, knowing that your choices reflect your authentic self.

Meditation also connects destiny with purpose. Many people drift through life without a sense of purpose, chasing goals that do not fulfill them. Meditation helps you discover your purpose by connecting you with the Someone Within You. This inner self knows your strengths, your passions, your values. It whispers your calling, reminding you of the contribution you are meant to make. Purpose is not always grand or dramatic, it may be simple yet profound raising a family, creating art, serving others, living with kindness. Meditation ensures that your destiny is shaped by purpose, not by chance. It transforms life from a series of random events into a meaningful journey.

Destiny is also shaped by freedom, and meditation cultivates freedom by releasing attachment. Much of life's suffering comes from attachment to outcomes, possessions, identities, or expectations. These attachments create fear and limit growth. Meditation teaches you to release attachment, to live in the present, to trust the flow of life. This freedom ensures that your destiny is not constrained by fear but expanded by openness. You begin to see destiny not as a rigid path but as a living journey, full of possibilities.

Meditation also reveals that destiny is shared. While it is deeply personal, it is also connected to others. Your choices affect not only your life but the lives of those around you. Meditation deepens your awareness of this interconnectedness. It teaches you compassion, reminding you that your destiny is not isolated but part of a larger whole. This awareness ensures that your destiny is not selfish but inclusive, not isolated but connected. It transforms destiny from personal achievement into collective contribution.

Ultimately, meditation teaches that destiny is not imposed from outside but shaped from within. It is not a script written by fate but a story written by your choices. Meditation ensures that you are the author of this story, guided by the Someone Within You. It reminds you that destiny is not about becoming someone else but about meeting the authentic self who has always been there.

In closing, meditation and destiny are inseparable. Meditation is the practice that ensures your destiny is authentic, purposeful, resilient, and free. It is the dialogue that guides your path, the compass that directs your choices, the strength that sustains your journey. Destiny is not something waiting at the end of life, it is something created in every moment of awareness. Meditation ensures that this creation reflects your truth, your values, and your purpose. It transforms destiny from mystery into clarity, from chance into choice, from accident into authenticity. And in this transformation, you discover that destiny is not something you find but something you create, guided by the Someone Within You.

Obstacles and Misunderstanding in Meditation

Meditation is often portrayed as a serene practice where one sits quietly, closes the eyes, and instantly finds peace. Yet anyone who has truly attempted meditation knows that the path is not always smooth. It is filled with obstacles, misunderstandings, and moments of doubt. These challenges are not signs of failure, they are part of the journey. In fact, they are the very material through which meditation teaches us patience, resiliencc, and self-understanding. To explore meditation deeply, we must acknowledge these obstacles and clarify the misunderstandings that surround the practice.

One of the most common obstacles is **restlessness of the mind**. The moment you sit in silence, thoughts rush in like waves. You remember unfinished tasks, replay conversations, or worry about the future. Many beginners assume that meditation requires the complete elimination of thoughts, and when they cannot achieve this, they feel defeated. This is a misunderstanding. Meditation is not about erasing thoughts but about changing your relationship with them. The restless mind is natural, it reflects the momentum of daily life. Through meditation, you learn to observe these thoughts without being carried away. You begin to see them as passing clouds rather than permanent realities. The obstacle of restlessness becomes the lesson of detachment.

Another obstacle is **doubt**. People often wonder: *Am I doing this right? Is this working? Will I ever feel calm?* Doubt arises because meditation does not always provide immediate results. Unlike physical exercise, where effort produces visible changes, meditation works subtly. Its effects accumulate over time, often unnoticed until one day you realize you are calmer, more patient, or more resilient. The misunderstanding here is the belief that meditation must produce instant peace. In truth, meditation is a relationship, not a transaction. Like any relationship, it requires trust, persistence, and openness. Doubt is natural, but it can be overcome by consistency. Each session, even if it feels unproductive, is a step toward deeper connection with the inner self.

Distraction is another obstacle. The world is full of noise phones buzzing, responsibilities calling, environments demanding attention. Even within silence, the mind finds ways to distract itself. Beginners often feel frustrated, believing that distraction means failure. But distraction is not failure, it is part of the process. Meditation teaches you to notice distraction and gently return to awareness. Each return strengthens your focus, like a muscle being exercised. The misunderstanding lies in expecting uninterrupted concentration. In reality, meditation is the practice of returning, again and again, to the present moment. Each return is success, not failure.

Physical discomfort can also be an obstacle. Sitting still for long periods may cause stiffness, pain, or fatigue. Many assume that meditation requires perfect posture, and when they cannot achieve it, they feel inadequate. This is a misunderstanding. Posture matters less than presence. Meditation is not about forcing the body into rigid positions but about finding comfort that allows awareness to flourish. If sitting cross-legged is painful, sit on a chair. If stillness is difficult, begin with shorter sessions. The obstacle of discomfort becomes the lesson of compassion learning to treat your body with kindness rather than demand.

Another misunderstanding is the belief that meditation is an escape from life. Some imagine it as a retreat into silence, away from responsibilities and challenges. But meditation is not about avoidance it is about engagement. It teaches you to enter life more deeply, with clarity and calm. The obstacle here is the tendency to use meditation as a way to bypass emotions or problems. True meditation does not bypass, it confronts. It allows you to face emotions honestly, to listen to your inner voice, and to act with wisdom. It is not about escaping the world but about living in it with awareness.

Impatience is another obstacle. In a world of instant gratification, people expect meditation to deliver quick results. When progress feels slow, they abandon the practice. The misunderstanding is the belief that meditation is a technique with measurable outcomes. In truth, meditation is a journey without destination. Its value lies not in reaching a goal but in walking the path. Impatience reveals our attachment to results, meditation teaches us to release that attachment. The obstacle of impatience becomes the lesson of patience, reminding us that growth unfolds in its own time.

Cultural misconceptions also create obstacles. Some believe meditation belongs only to certain religions or traditions, and therefore hesitate to practice it. Others assume it requires chanting, rituals, or complex techniques. These misunderstandings limit access to meditation's universal benefits. Meditation is not confined to any culture, it is a human practice, available to all. It is simply the art of awareness, the act of listening to the inner self. Rituals may enrich it, but they are not essential. The obstacle of cultural misunderstanding becomes the lesson of openness, reminding us that truth transcends boundaries.

Another subtle obstacle is **fear of silence**. For many, silence feels uncomfortable, even threatening. It exposes emotions, memories, and truths that have been buried. Meditation brings these to the surface, and the experience can be unsettling. The misunderstanding is the belief that silence should always feel peaceful. In reality, silence is honest. It reveals what has been hidden, whether joy or pain. Facing this honesty requires courage. Meditation teaches you to embrace silence, to trust that even discomfort is part of healing. The obstacle of fear becomes the lesson of courage.

Finally, one of the greatest misunderstandings is the belief that meditation is about becoming someone else more spiritual, more enlightened, more perfect. This belief creates pressure and discouragement. In truth, meditation is not about becoming someone else but about meeting the Someone Within You. It is about recognizing the authentic self that has always been present. The obstacle of striving becomes the lesson of acceptance. Meditation teaches you that you are already whole, already complete, already worthy.

In conclusion, obstacles and misunderstandings are not barriers to meditation, they are the very material through which meditation teaches. Restlessness teaches detachment, doubt teaches trust, distraction teaches focus, discomfort teaches compassion, impatience teaches patience, fear teaches courage, and misunderstanding teaches clarity. Each obstacle is a messenger, delivering lessons from the inner self. Meditation is not about avoiding these challenges but about embracing them, learning from them, and growing through them. When you understand this, you realize that obstacles are not signs of failure but signs of progress. They are the stepping stones that lead you deeper into dialogue with the Someone Within You, shaping your growth and destiny.

Prayer and Surrender

Prayer and surrender are two of the most powerful ways to connect with your inner self, and when explained in simple, direct language, they become practices anyone can understand and apply. Think of this as a conversation between us, where I'm guiding you step by step into what these ideas mean and how they can transform your life.

Prayer, at its heart, is simply talking. It's not about memorizing long verses or following strict rituals unless those things help you personally. It's about expressing what's inside you your hopes, your worries, your gratitude, or even your confusion. When you pray, you're opening a dialogue with the part of you that listens quietly, the part that knows your deepest truths. You don't need to be formal. You can say, "I'm scared," or "I'm thankful," or even just sit in silence and let your feelings rise. That is prayer. It's a way of giving voice to your emotions so they don't stay locked inside. And when you do this, you'll often find that clarity begins to appear, because speaking to your inner self is like shining a light into a dark room you start to see what was hidden.

But prayer alone isn't enough. That's where surrender comes in. Surrender means letting go of the need to control every outcome. It's not about giving up, it's about trusting. Imagine planting a seed in the soil. You can water it, give it sunlight, and care for it, but you can't force it to grow faster. You have to trust the process. That's surrender. It's the willingness to say, "I've done my part, now I'll let life take care of the rest." This doesn't mean you stop trying or caring. It means you stop exhausting yourself by clinging to things you can't control. Surrender brings peace because it allows you to rest in the flow of life instead of fighting against it.

Prayer and surrender work best when they're practiced together. Prayer is you speaking, surrender is you listening. Prayer is asking, surrender is trusting. If you only pray, you might end up demanding or worrying about whether your words are heard. If you only surrender, you might feel passive, like you're not expressing yourself. But when you combine them, you create balance. You say what's in your heart, and then you let go of the outcome. It's like breathing: prayer is the inhale, surrender is the exhale. Both are necessary to stay alive, and both are necessary to stay at peace.

Let's look at how this works in daily life. Suppose you're facing a tough decision. You might pray by saying, "I want clarity, I don't know what to do." That's you expressing your need. Then you surrender by saying, "I'll wait for the right sign, I don't need to rush." Or imagine you're struggling with weakness. You might pray for strength, but surrender allows you to accept that weakness is part of growth. You might pray for success, but surrender helps you trust that even failure can teach you something valuable. In this way, surrender doesn't cancel prayer it deepens it. It turns prayer from a demand into a dialogue, from a transaction into a relationship with your inner self.

Prayer and surrender also help during emotional storms. When you're angry, sad, or overwhelmed, prayer gives you a way to release those feelings instead of bottling them up. You can say, "I'm hurting, I need peace." That's prayer. Then surrender helps you pause, breathe, and not react immediately. Sometimes just saying, "I don't know what to do, but I trust it will be okay," is enough to calm your mind. This combination prevents emotions from controlling you. Prayer gives them a voice, surrender gives them space to settle.

Over time, practicing prayer and surrender builds a relationship with your inner person. You start to feel less alone, because you realize there's always a part of you listening, guiding, and supporting. You begin to notice that answers don't always come in words they come in feelings, in sudden clarity, in small signs around you. You might feel lighter after prayer, or notice that surrender brings unexpected solutions. This is your inner self responding. The more you practice, the stronger this connection becomes.

Philosophically, prayer and surrender reflect the balance of life itself. Prayer affirms your ability to act, to express, to desire. Surrender affirms your ability to trust, to release, to accept. Together, they teach that freedom doesn't come from controlling everything, but from participating fully while also letting go. You act, but you also allow. You speak, but you also listen. You plant, but you also trust the soil. This balance is wisdom it's the recognition that life is both gift and responsibility, both mystery and revelation.

In times of crisis, this balance becomes even more important. When the mind is overwhelmed, prayer provides expression, a way to release the weight of emotions. Surrender provides relief, a way to rest in trust when solutions seem impossible. Together, they prevent despair from consuming you. They remind you that even in darkness, there is light within. The inner person, accessed through prayer and surrender, becomes a source of resilience. You discover that strength is not the absence of struggle but the ability to trust amidst struggle. Prayer gives voice to your pain, surrender gives peace to your heart. This dual practice transforms suffering into growth, chaos into clarity.

Think of prayer and surrender as daily practices, not one-time acts. They can be woven into ordinary moments. A short prayer of gratitude in the morning, a moment of surrender before sleep. A whispered prayer before a meeting, a quiet surrender when things don't go as planned. These small acts build a habit of inner communication. They turn solitude into sanctuary, and they make everyday life feel more meaningful.

So, to put it simply prayer is your voice, surrender is your trust. Prayer is planting the seed, surrender is letting it grow. Prayer is effort, surrender is peace. Together, they help you connect with your inner person in a way that feels natural, comforting, and powerful. They teach you that the deepest answers are not found outside but within, in the quiet communion between your conscious self and your inner self. And once you learn to practice both, you'll find that life feels lighter, clearer, and more balanced.

Message from the Author:

Dear Reader,

If you are reading this page, it means you have completed the book. I hope you have understood the concept of SOMEONE WITHIN YOU the idea that we all carry a person inside us whom we should admire and rely on, rather than depending too much on others.

There are many ways to discover your inner self and continue to grow. But the most important step is to recognize and truly feel the power we all carry within.

I wish you the very best on your journey of transformation, as you uncover a new, better, and ultimately the best version of yourself.

Acknowledgement

To all readers, thank you. Writing the first book of my journey has been a wholesome and transformative experience. It made me feel part of a larger author community, where I learned something new every day. The discipline required to write consistently has shaped me in ways I never expected.

I want to thank my friend who is also co-author of this book, **Anushka.K** .The overall idea of writing this book came to me because of her. There was a time when I loved reading books, I would always end up at book festivals searching for new ones. One day, while reading, I observed a pattern within myself which was inner person and I shared this idea with her. After our conversation, a thought struck me: I am always reading books, but what if I write one? Thinking is never a big task for humans, but execution is the hardest part. As this was going to be my first book, I gathered information, but my motivation suddenly dropped to zero after seeing the process. Once again, after talking with her, she supported and encouraged me to start writing. She herself became a source of motivation for me, so I did not quit midway through my journey. If you are reading this book today, it is largely because of her. Thank you, **Anushka.K**

With the New Year came a new person into my life an author **Divya.Chauhan** who had already published her own books. Through her, I learned many new things that I did not know, as I am new to this author community. Publishing a book, printing a book, editing a book, all these things, which I am going to face for the first time in the future, filled my mind with questions. But this author made it simple for me. Thank you, **Divya.Chauhan** for the guidance and all information your provided was helpful for me.

This acknowledgement goes to that inspiring author, co-author and to you dear readers, whose presence has made this book possible. Writing was never easy but if you have these kind of people in life everything feels easy. Together, you remind me that writing is not just a solitary act, but a shared experience that connects hearts and minds across time.

www.ingramcontent.com/pod-product-compliance
Ingram Content Group UK Ltd.
Pitfield, Milton Keynes, MK11 3LW, UK
UKHW021402190726
13845UKWH00028B/820